How to
Write Fast
UNDER PRESSURE

How to
Write Fast
UNDER PRESSURE

Philip Vassallo

⊁AMACOM

American Management Association

New York • Atlanta • Brussels • Chicago • Mexico City • San Francisco
Shanghai • Tokyo • Toronto • Washington, D.C.

This publication is designed to provide accurate and authoritative information in regard to the subject matter covered. It is sold with the understanding that the publisher is not engaged in rendering legal, accounting, or other professional service. If legal advice or other expert assistance is required, the services of a competent professional person should be sought.

Library of Congress Cataloging-in-Publication Data

Vassallo, Philip.
    How to write fast under pressure / Philip Vassallo.
        p.   cm.
    Includes bibliographical references and index.
    ISBN-13: 978-0-8144-1485-9
    ISBN-10: 0-8144-1485-0
    1. Business writing.   2. Authorship.   I. Title.

    HF5718.3.V368   2010
    651.7'4—dc22
                                        2009011228

Printing number

10 9 8 7 6 5 4 3 2 1

For Elizabeth Vassallo-DeLuca:

daughter, sister, wife, friend,
creator, organizer, adviser, healer

Contents

Acknowledgments

Writers must be solitary creatures when plying their trade, yet they do so as human beings. They are social animals. The kind of work I do as a writer requires me to spend hours alone, and the work I do as a teacher demands that I spend an equal amount of time in contact with students who, for the most part, will end their relationship with me the second the course is over. Since the activities that consume most of my time do not fulfill my desire to be in the company of people with whom I share an enduring relationship, the folks I write about here cannot imagine how grateful I am to have had them involved with me during my work on this book.

From the American Management Association (AMA), I am first indebted to Richard Bradley, Portfolio Manager extraordinaire, without whom this book would not even have been on my radar screen. He asked me to design a new AMA course titled "How to Write Fast When It's Due Yesterday." Richard's visionary approach to almost everything he does, his respect for everyone he meets, and his playfulness about every place he finds himself make him a unique soul. I thank him for the nourishment of his faith in my knowledge and in my ability to get the job done. I am also grateful for Ellen Kadin, Executive Editor of AMACOM Books, who gave me the green light for this book. Her approval has been encouraging and her patience downright inspiring. William R. Helms III, AMACOM Editorial Assistant, offered numerous suggestions for improving both the substance and style of this book. Working with him made me comfortable in knowing that some ambiguity would be clarified, clichés would be nuanced, and miscues would be caught. Copy editor Jerilyn Famighetti proved invaluable during the line editing phase of the production process. Her ability to strike a balance between grammatical convention and elegant expression made this book better than it would otherwise have been. My appreciation also goes to Ed Fields, longtime AMA faculty member and professor of financial management at Baruch College, who graciously introduced me to AMA and whose influence got me in the door.

Needless to say, many others outside AMA have contributed to this book as well. I am indebted to my wife, Georgia, for everything I've been able to do since we met in 1975. She has played a huge part in all of it. Where those things went well, I know she was there; where things didn't go as planned, if only I had relied more on her amazing insights. My older daughter, Elizabeth De-Luca, to whom I dedicate this book, and my son-in-law, Dr. Darrow DeLuca, are always a visit away if I want the education that their medical studies can offer or the inspiration that their everloving kindness can bring. My younger daughter, Helen Vassallo, a music educator, performer, composer, conductor, and artist, continues to amaze me with her capacity for hard work and her insight into the human condition. To my sister, Elizabeth Hitz, who was and always will be my first English teacher, what can I say for all the good you have brought to my life? How thankful I am for the life of Danielle Babo, who proofread several of my manuscripts for me as I prepared this book. In her brief time in the flesh, she extended my definition of courage, and her spiritual presence continues to inspire me.

Acknowledgments

To the countless students who have challenged me to come up with better solutions to their writing problems, the numerous writers and teachers who have educated me in finding those solutions, and the organizations that have asked me to provide those solutions—where would I be without you?

DASH—Getting to the Task

You're at your desk writing a proposal for a key client—a project your boss has just dumped on you and that was due yesterday because he sat on it all week. Meanwhile, all you can think of is that sales report your boss's boss expects on her desk from you by the end of the business day. You can't finish that project because one of your teammates hasn't run the month-end operating expenses that you need to analyze in the report. The e-mail inbox shows 14 new messages in the past 20 minutes. The electricians are snaking cable through the ceiling tiles, conjuring the image of a pack of rats burrowing through an overhead tunnel. Someone walks past you with his mobile phone blaring the *William Tell Overture*. Two colleagues whose work areas are nowhere near yours have decided to set up camp right in front of your area to argue over what picture should win the next Academy Award. It's past two o'clock and you haven't eaten anything all day. It doesn't help that a nagging migraine makes your head feel like it's going to explode. The computer monitor becomes increasingly blurred. An incoming fax screeches its way through the machine rollers. The photocopier down the hall is pounding incessantly. The road department is drilling on the street right outside your window, and you're sure the vibration of those jackhammers rates at least a 7.0 on the Richter Scale. An incoherent announcement screaming through the intercom—something about ignoring the intermittent howling of the fire alarm—makes you imagine some infathomable fingernail torture. In come 11 more e-mails—most of which you're sure have nothing to do with you, but which you must open just in case they are for you. You remember that you have to get back to two vendors, three clients, and four teammates about a major engagement that affects everyone's timeline. A manager saunters by and says, "Since you seem to have some time on your hands, would you mind helping me carry these cartons into the storage room?" Before you can indignantly say, "Excuse me," in walks a vice president asking, "Do you have a copy of yesterday's meeting review? I can't seem to find mine." You turn beet red and erupt in a primal howl: "Arghhhhhhhhhhhhhh!"

If you've read the previous paragraph with the distinct feeling that you've been-there-done-that and that you can use some help in dealing with such situations, then you're reading the right book. *How to Write Fast Under Pressure* focuses on dealing with time pressures resulting from writing in all sorts of situations and in all kinds of environments—especially when the writing is due yesterday!

Work-Related Writing Situations

Far more people actually write for a living than they'd care to admit—or realize. You *do* write for a living if you spend most of your workday at the computer as your brain directs your fingers to request, respond, report, explain, analyze, evaluate, justify, troubleshoot, summarize, or propose. True, you might not fancy yourself a writer in the sense of being a novelist, playwright, news reporter, or biographer; however, you actually spend as much of your day processing words as any of these writers.

In fact, you might have far greater demands on your time than the so-called professionals. Perhaps you manage multiple writing tasks for varied readers, creating proposals for a steering committee whose members represent diverse interest groups, such as Production, Sales, Purchasing, and Finance. Or maybe you write root-cause analyses that need to pass through Operations, System Safety, and Internal Audit, all of which have unique concerns about business affecting events. Or you might have to crunch a 40-page audit report into a 250-word, one-page summary for review by the chief executive officer, chief operating officer, chief financial officer, and chief information officer—each one wanting a different 250 words! Regardless of the situation, few employees get a lot of time to craft such documents—they must write them on the fly.

Other challenging writing moments pop up whenever we're not writing strictly by ourselves. For instance, writing for the boss's signature demands a lot of reflection on style. The last time you wrote for her, she expected you to take an aggressive approach, but this time she's asking you to pull back the reins. Sometimes she cautions you about using too much passive voice, but now she wants the exact passive style that you've tried so hard to avoid. What's going on here? Such a situation can create confusion or, worse, shake your confidence and cause you to run behind schedule.

Writing collaboratively can lead to heaps of trouble, as well. Say your manager has assigned you to write the introduction and conclusion of a lengthy report, and he has pegged two of your teammates to write the body. You may feel virtually helpless until their completed sections come to you, so if they're behind schedule, the time pressures on you will be huge. Making matters worse are the divergent writing styles that each teammate may use, triggering the natural tendency in you to deal with that discrepancy by editing for consistency of style before you even start on your writing task. Those early visions of perfection you harbored quickly become overshadowed by the specter of mediocrity—and you haven't yet written your first word!

Writing Environments

Let's face it: You are not living in a writer-friendly world. Human and artificial noises come to you in surround sound. The eyesores of clutter created by an office mate or, admittedly, by you yourself distract you from looking at a new writing task with a fresh pair of eyes. The office is crowded with folders, coffee cups, and keys belonging to no one and with people who shouldn't be there. How can you meet deadlines in such daunting circumstances?

The mess of modern times is especially brutal on travelers, who try to get their writing done in public places like restaurants, buses, and trains or in air, rail, and bus terminals. Those loud mobile-phone conversations, incoherent public-address announcements, screaming music, and 50-inch TV screens screeching pointless words from pitchmen and pundits plague you wherever you go. You can't wait to get to your hotel room, where you'll really have some quality quiet time to write. But by the time you check in and unpack your suitcase for that one-night stay, you surrender to the overwhelming temptation to turn on the TV and lie in bed for the rest of the night. You know that no time is better than now to knock off that proposal or report, yet you long for a good night's sleep. Yes, the sandman beckons, and, what the heck, no one's watching. You're human, aren't you?

The Need for a Sensible Approach to Writing Fast

This book aims to provide you with useful solutions to break through writer's block, jumpstart the writing process, and stoke your creative flame. If you just can't get started quickly enough, here you will find the tools to start writing right away. If you struggle through drafts, you will learn plenty of useful tips to write quicker than you already do. If you tend to put off writing assignments until the last moment, only to lament the quality of your finished draft, you'll have a greater awareness of yourself to become more proactive—not only to get started sooner but also to anticipate and strategize for future projects that have yet to be assigned to you. These sound like huge claims, and they are. But they all depend less on this book than on you. The ideas in this book have worked for many people, including me, but you have to use them and have the right attitude when trying them.

Think for a minute about what it really means to write fast. What are we looking for in a fast writer? Words-per-minute typed? I doubt it. If we were, then professional typists and stenographers would be the fastest writers. Of course, some of them are fast writers, but I have met many who are not. That's because typists and stenographers are copyists. They do not have to generate original ideas; they're just repeating with their fingers what they've seen with their eyes or heard with their ears. When they have to create their own ideas, however, their word-per-minute count drops significantly, even the best of them.

As a case in point, an administrative assistant once told me (let's call her Carmen) that she can type 90 words per minute but still has a hard time getting started when she's on her own, and she wanted to know why. I explained to her that one thing has nothing to do with the other. Let's do some simple math by looking at

5

Carmen's typical workday. She works nine to five, minus an hour for lunch and two 15-minute breaks. That leaves us with six and a half hours. Let's discount another 30 minutes for the rest room, stretch breaks, natural fatigue, and idle chatter about the latest reality TV show, ballgame, movie, or work-related gossip. That brings down the productive work time to six hours, or 360 minutes. At 90 words a minute, 360 minutes yield 32,400 words, or the length of a short novel, in one workday. Moving along, if she works 240 days a year as most of us do (365 days in the year less 104 for weekends, 10 for vacation, 8 for holidays, and 3 personal or sick days), then she's typing 7,776,000 words a year, or 195 novel-length books a year!

Sounds absurd, doesn't it? You bet! Counting words is one thing, but producing them steadily is another. After these mind-numbing numbers sunk into Carmen's reality, she exclaimed, "Gimme a break!" No one types that fast. And we write a whole lot slower, believe me. The truth is that we don't reach anywhere near those kinds of numbers on any given day.

The issue of writing fast is far more complicated than dealing with sheer volume. For instance, an e-mail might take a half hour, and two reports might take five minutes, depending on the content, complexity, audience, and situation. In many people's work, there's no such thing as an average e-mail, letter, or proposal. Writing fast is not about typing fast; it's about clearing your mind so that you can write as easily as you speak. Writing may not seem at all natural to you. After all, when we were at the evolutionary stage of walking on all fours, the ape in us saw our hands as a means of grabbing food for sustenance, punching our enemies for self-preservation, and feeling along the cave walls in the dark for safety. Then, some five thousand years ago, those imaginative Sumerians committed us to using our hands for creating permanent representations of our thoughts with their cuneiform, and we've never been the same since. Suddenly, we all became capable of "literacy."

After five millennia, writing is natural, so much so that we have even adapted to instruments dependent on motor skills far finer than the hammer and chisel: pens, pencils, typewriter keys, keyboards, and pocket-size electronic devices. Like it or not, writing is so natural that it has replaced speaking in many situations—and we love it, even those of us who say we hate it. We send text messages, e-mails, and instant messages to our friends, families, and coworkers, and we enjoy the 24-7 availability of the Internet and the control we have over when and how and with whom we interact online, which electronic shopping cart we fill, which Web site questionnaire and application we can complete, and how we can get everything we missed during a rush-hour commute by viewing the same information on a 4-ounce, 2 × 4-inch BlackBerry or iPhone.

Now that many companies give their staff all these amazing tech tools, such as laptops and BlackBerrys, they exact a steep price for these "gifts": greater availability and speed. Now there are no excuses. You have the tools, so get it done. The problem with this thinking is that more messages flood our laps and palms than we can reasonably handle with perfect quality. Efficiency supersedes quality in these situations. This is not necessarily a good thing, but it is what it is, and trying to stop the flow of messages is like a child's attempt at emptying the ocean with his pail at the beach. Anxiety about writing is wasted time. Writing is not about cogitating; it's about writing. It's not about thinking of doing it but about doing it.

Having the Right Frame of Mind: The Fable of Mopey Moe and Speedy Didi

Meet Mopey Moe, a sad sack who has just gotten a job on the strength of his technical skills at WeCanDoIt Enterprises, a growing business. He knows how to talk the talk of his profession, but when it comes to writing, poor Moe is the sort of guy who laments, "I can't write fast enough . . . I'll get around to it sooner or later . . . If I do nothing, maybe this writing assignment will just go away . . . Writing just isn't my thing . . . Writing this is killing me . . . They'll tear this apart . . . I feel like such a waste!" On his second week at the job, he is staring at a blank computer monitor in front of him, and the e-mails are flowing into his inbox nonstop. He wonders how to answer one from an internal client whose one question causes him to ask two or three questions of his own. He probably should forward it to his boss, but she said in his interview that she would trust him to handle these situations on his own, so he doesn't want to appear weak by asking her for help. In fact, she noted that the last person in the position should have been more assertive, independent, and proactive. Moe has her point front-stage-center in his mind. Now that he thinks of it, his failure to be proactive by using e-mail to troubleshoot issues in his last job probably caused most of those client complaints. Raising this matter with his boss would get him on the path toward career suicide. But if he does the right thing by asking the client an additional two or three questions to better understand his situation, how long will the client take before getting back to him? Maybe the client will go to someone else to solve his problem. There goes his value to the team and organization down the drain! Worst of all, maybe the client will write Moe's boss to complain about how uncooperative, inefficient, and thoughtless Moe is, just like the last guy WeCan-DoIt hired.

Stop! Moe, you've just wasted valuable minutes of your time doing nothing! A few more of these moments over the next few e-mails turn into huge chunks of time—minutes turning into hours—of unproductive fretting over a workweek. That's where the writing time is going, Mopey Moe, and you know it. You are actually talking yourself out of doing your job successfully. The reason you're sitting at a computer all day is that you're a full-time writer, like it or not. If you don't like it, then sell ice cream on a truck or install cable lines. There's nothing wrong with those jobs, but if you want to stick around, then get over yourself and get started writing—whenever, wherever, and however you can.

What does this scene have to do with writing fast at work? Everything. What we do when we're not writing matters a great deal to our writing efficiency. Meditate on writing, pray on it, daydream your way to writing productivity—whatever it takes. That's what this book is all about: using all you've got to improve your writing speed. It's not about improving your grammar, style, and organization. I'll assume that you know a well-written document when you see it, one that is purposeful, complete, organized, courteous, clear, concise, and correct. And if you know one when you see one, then you can write one when you need one. You'll find a few examples of good writing in this book and in many other business writing and technical writing books, but the focus here is on the *how* and not the *what*, on the process of writing and not the product of writing, on what it takes within your own mind and around your environment to manage your small writing tasks and big writing projects thoroughly, consistently, and quickly. The one thing you have in common with the best and the worst writers you've ever met is time. You have talent, too, but what you may lack in talent you can make up for by using your time wisely.

Now meet Speedy Didi, Mopey Moe's boss. Unlike Mopey Moe, who puts things off, Didi gets things done. She simply says, "I'll write this now," and then she does what she says. While Mopey Moe has no plan for getting his writing done, Didi does. On demand, she can always articulate her path to the end of a document. Moe drafts slowly and painstakingly; Didi is known for exclaiming, "What's writing but a bunch of words!" She does not attach any undue reverence to the writing task. She scoffs at images of the noble but starving writer so selflessly advancing profound thoughts for the betterment of mankind. Where Moe lacks the vigor to get to the end of his draft, Speedy Didi possesses apparently boundless energy. "Why stop now?" she'll insist. She counters Moe's sense of discouragement with an optimistic can-do attitude. Even though she is not the greatest writer in the world and has a writing weakness or two of her own, she will always say, "I can write" to whoever asks. She's utterly fearless in the face of any writing task, including those she's never attempted. "If other people have done these assignments, then so can I," she concludes.

What Didi has is priceless: an indomitable spirit, adventurous disposition, and unflagging curiosity. She has a deeply grounded sense of reality. She thinks—no, she knows—she can take on anything life throws her way. She looks at the unknown with an immediate awareness, based on experience, that the future will soon become known to her. And Didi likes new challenges because she believes she's bound to learn from them.

Is Didi a flawless writer? What a question! Of course not! How can she be when neither you nor I could agree on what makes a flawless writer or piece of writing? I might prefer T. S. Eliot to your Virginia Woolf. I might think the world of *The Catcher in the Rye*, a novel you just can't get into; I might spend all night reading twentieth-century American poetry, and you might wonder why on earth I would want to do such a thing. My writing masters might be your utter bores, and your favorite books might be a waste of my time. One thing Speedy Didi knows for sure is that the idea of what makes good writing is a subjective judgment. She knows she's not a perfect writer; in fact, she's one of average ability. But the trick is that, while she takes seriously other people's opinions of her writing ability as a gauge to measure the improvement of her finished drafts, she doesn't let their opinions paralyze her and keep her from writing efficiently or, worse, let them cause her to retreat into a shell of self-absorbed defeat. She knows that writing could be hard at times, but so is cleaning her house on Saturday, trying to comfort a squealing infant, or dealing with an upset client who acts like an infant. So Didi does incorrectly drop an *s* or *ed* from word endings at times, and she might not always have the perfect sentence structure under pressure-packed situations. And sometimes she misplaces or conceals the point of her message. She's human. But Speedy Didi never misses a deadline. That's why she would be your and my go-to person to get a writing job done.

Myth Busting: The Myths and the Realities of Writing

Like anything else, writing at work is laden with its own myths. Mopey Moe knows them all—and he believes them, he makes them real: "Writing this is impossible . . . Writing this is going to kill me . . . I can't write with that person . . . I can't write for this boss . . . No one likes anything I write" (see Figure 1-1).

Why call them myths? Because each of these five statements cannot possibly be true. Let's take them one at a time. First, writing something at work can be done; writing assignments get done all the time. Second, writing is not literally going to kill anyone, not even Mopey Moe. Third, two people working in the same company can always find ways in common to collaborate on a writing assignment, no matter how small those ways may be. Fourth, no matter how demanding a boss Didi is, she has to accept some things or else nothing would ever get done. Finally, someone has to at least tolerate Moe's writing; otherwise, he would never be assigned anything to write and would have been fired from all his

11

previous jobs. Come to think of it, he might get fired if his mopey attitude persists. The net effect of these myths is a self-fulfilling prophecy leading to a lack of writing proficiency, general incompetence on the job, and bad work relationships.

FIGURE 1-1: Writing Myths and Realities

Myth	*Reality*
"I never have enough time to write."	"I make every minute count."
"I'll get around to it sooner or later."	"I'll write this now."
"If I do nothing, maybe it will just go away."	"Here's the path to the end."
"I need the perfect atmosphere to write."	"I create my own atmosphere."
"I can't write fast enough."	"It's just a bunch of words."
"Writing this is killing me."	"I can write!"
"They'll tear it apart."	"I'll get this done."
"I feel like such a waste!"	"Why stop now?"

The converse of all these statements is, in fact, the truth. Writing anything that the job requires is possible, even those assignments that require a lot of time. Far from being detrimental to one's well-being, writing is good for you in the sense that it cultivates sound thinking and develops your skills. Writing with others is a great way to build strong relationships by placing you in situations where you can teach and learn from each other, share an otherwise heavy workload, and get another viewpoint on the effectiveness of what you're writing. Writing for a demanding boss, if we assume that the boss knows what she's doing, affords a rare opportunity to improve the caliber of your writing. Even a boss who isn't even half the writer that the subordinate is (my experience tells me this is often the case) still sees the document from the higher perspective of its place in the organization, which calls for a more acute understanding of style and a deeper awareness of the reader's concerns. And, as for people liking your writing, what does that mean, anyway? So many people I know don't like and would never read the works of Thomas Mann, William Faulkner, Samuel Beckett, or Harold Pinter—yet all of them won the Nobel Prize for literature! As long as you like your writing, what should you care about what others think? Better yet, maybe you shouldn't like your writing so much so that you commit to improving it constantly!

At this point, you might be wondering what possessed Speedy Didi to hire Mopey Moe in the first place. More about that later, but for now the short answer is this: Didi is an optimist. She has confidence that Moe can change once he's learned a tip or two. If he can become so technically proficient at his job that she would hate to have a competitor get a hold of him, then he can become a good enough writer under pressure to communicate his knowledge to his clients. He'll learn a tip or two of the many described in this book to overcome his counterproductive idiosyncrasies and negative attitude. So will you by the time you're finished with this book.

Getting Motivated: The Treat and the Trick

While we're on the subject of myth busting, think about a time when you did get some piece of writing done on time. Think small: It doesn't have to be a doctoral dissertation, book proposal, white paper, employee handbook, or user manual. It could be something as small as a routine monthly half-page status report for your team, a six-line e-mail providing instructions to a teammate, or a meeting agenda for a client. Reflect for a moment on that on-time submission. That's the question Speedy Didi puts to Mopey Moe:

Didi: I'm sure you can think of one time that you really nailed down a writing assignment.

Moe: Can't say I remember one time in my life when that was the case.

Didi: Come on. There has to be at least one time in your entire life.

Moe: Can you give me a hint?

Didi: Moe, it's your life, not mine.

Moe: Well, I get out most of my quick-response e-mails pretty quickly.

Didi: There you have it.

Moe: But that's *e-mail*, not *writing*.

Didi: If e-mail is not writing, then tell me what it is.

Moe: (*pause*) OK. But it's not *hard* writing.

Didi: So start thinking of all the writing you do around here as not hard.

Moe: Just because I say it's not hard doesn't make it so.

Didi: Then why should the reverse be true, that just because you say it is, it is?

Moe: Huh?

Didi: Listen. Think small. You've got a lot of technical skills, so I'm sure heaps of managers have depended on you to write root-cause analyses, trip reports, justifications. . . .

Moe: Yeah, and they tear it apart and get all huffy about my style.

Didi: Lab reviews, product specifications, meeting minutes. . . .

Moe: Yeah, minutes! There was that one time I got those dreadful minutes done in the nick of time. . . .

Even Moe has submitted a lot of his writing on time or ahead of schedule. Although Moe isn't inclined to consider his successes and would rather dwell on what he sees as his failures, even he can think of that one time that he wrote those mind-bending meeting minutes for the production team at his last job—on time. He hated the idea that because he was the lowest ranking person at that meeting, the managers would pull their weight and defer all meeting reporting responsibilities to him. That's often the problem with writing meeting minutes. The person assigned to writing them often has the least authority and is the least informed; as a result, he struggles with knowing whether to include certain information in the minutes, especially if it is politically charged. Yet Moe clearly recalls he wrote a three-page review of an all-morning meeting involving 12 members of the production, marketing, and sales teams. The meeting involved seven agenda items concerning three major projects, and seven of the attendees were department heads who gave presentations. Moe had to cover all those issues, projects, and presentations by describing the discussion points, project status, and required follow-up actions. For some skilled people, this writing task may not seem like an earth-shattering achievement, but for Moe it was a huge undertaking. He got it done before that business day was over. Sure, his boss made a bunch of changes in Moe's draft, but he got it done way before it was due.

Didi: Nice going. Must have felt good, huh?

Moe: You bet.

Didi: What did you do that worked?

Moe: Huh?

Didi: How did you pull it off?

Moe: I don't know.

Didi: It must have been something, because you were in rare form that day.

Moe: Oh, I remember! It was a Friday meeting and my last day before a once-in-a-lifetime, two-week vacation that I was going to start on Sunday. I figured if I didn't get it done before I left work that day, I'd have to slough through it on Saturday before I left. So I ate lunch at my desk, tuned out everyone and everything, didn't take calls or bounce back to too much e-mail, and just got the darn thing done, blemishes and all.

Didi: Do you notice how excited telling the story is making you feel?

Moe: Is it?

Didi: You seemed enthusiastic, confident, and determined that day, and you seem enthusiastic, confident, and determined in telling the story.

Moe: What's the point?

Didi: Attitude is half the battle. All you have to do is put the same sense of urgency in your daily writing that you put into that assignment a long time ago.

Moe: If I had that attitude, I'd burn out in a matter of days.

Didi: Not true. If you had that attitude, you'd be wide awake.

Moe: (*defensively*) I don't sleep on the job.

Didi: I know that. You do a good job. But you've been sleeping on this writing problem for way too long. Just keep thinking about the rewards for getting those writing jobs done. I call this the treat and the trick.

Moe: Treat and trick?

Didi: Yes. The treat is the reward: You got the writing job done on Friday so that you could enjoy Saturday without having to work and start vacation on Sunday with a clear mind. The trick: You tuned out the world and focused on the writing task as if it were the only thing in the world.

As a manager, Didi is worth her weight in diamond-studded gold. She's trying to get Moe started on a positive note by having Moe recollect an achievement, not a failure, and then to associate that achievement with principles of efficient writing, which she'll get to later. By getting Moe to think small instead of in grandiose terms, she's shattering established myths about good writing. She knows that discussing major writing accomplishments over prolonged periods makes it difficult to systematically break down the path toward the writing success. The greater accomplishments are nothing more than the smaller ones magnified, with the writer repeating the process successfully many times toward completion. Even if these huge achievements were easy to describe, they would likely intimidate less accomplished writers.

Understanding any writing success, knowing the treat and the trick behind it, dispels a time-wasting myth and proves a time-saving reality. When Moe admitted to his writing success of submitting those meeting minutes ahead of time (the treat) by getting started right away with one hundred percent focus on the task (the

FIGURE 1-2: Examples of the Treat and Trick

The Treat	→	The Trick
Andrew went into a meeting with a clear head.	→	He wrote three pressing request e-mails all within five minutes before he had to start a meeting.
Bette had an emergency report ready for her team as soon as she walked into the office.	→	She wrote the report on her laptop during a 20-minute subway ride into work.
Charlie cleaned up his e-mail inbox of 100 messages before leaving the office on Friday afternoon.	→	He didn't take calls, engage in office chat, or write anything but single-sentence response e-mails for 45 minutes so that he could focus purely on filing, forwarding, deleting, and responding to e-mails.
Danielle wrote the working and the revised drafts of a seven-page external proposal on the same day.	→	She wrote the first draft early in the morning—at her most creative time of day—and met with her boss in the early afternoon to give herself the needed revising time directly after the meeting.
Ed wrote three accident reports in the same time that his partner wrote one.	→	He cut-and-pasted most of the text from appropriate sections of previously written files; meanwhile, his partner tends to save few reports on her laptop, so she had to compose all her content from scratch.
Fran wrote 14 reply letters to customer inquiries or complaints while taking a dozen calls and responding to twice as many e-mails all in one morning.	→	She delegated the research on all the customer letters to Robert, a subordinate, who e-mailed the needed information to her, and she crafted the generic openings and closings of each letter while she was waiting for Bob's data.

trick), he contradicted every negative thing he has thought about his writing ability:

> Far from putting things off by saying "I'll get around to it sooner or later," he said, as Didi would, "I'll write this now."

> He saw the path to the end and blocked out the time to do

it, and he blocked out from his consciousness the procrastinator's credo: "If I do nothing, maybe it will just go away."

> ⟩ If he had moaned, "I can't write fast enough," he would have wasted his time wallowing in self-pity; instead, he played the hand he was dealt and thought, "It's just a bunch of words," and then produced them.

> ⟩ He didn't give himself a death sentence by crying, "Writing this is killing me," and he just focused on writing.

> ⟩ Even if "they'll tear this apart" entered his mind, his desire to go on vacation with a clean slate encouraged him to get the job done, to do his part in the editorial review process.

> ⟩ "I feel like such a waste" never entered his mind; the only waste he saw was time if he stopped his fingers from pounding the keyboard.

Getting in the right frame of mind is so important to people who for their whole lives have cried "I can't write" or "I hate writing." The treats and the tricks in Figure 1-2 and those you can think about yourself offer compelling and indisputable evidence that some things we often hear or say ourselves about writing just aren't true, while others are so deep in their truth that an awareness of them can empower us to write efficiently. The writing myths adversely affect our confidence to get the job done and erode the little time we have; the writing realities provide a great mindset for getting started and help maximize our composing time. Let's take the examples in Figure 1-2 one at a time:

> ⟩ When Andrew wrote three e-mails all within five minutes before his meeting, he dispelled the myth "I never have enough time to write" and proved the reality "I can make every minute count."

- In preparing that emergency report for her team during a brief subway ride, Bette smashed the myth "I need the perfect atmosphere to write" and embodied the reality "I create my own atmosphere."

- As Charlie was cleaning his e-mail inbox of a hundred messages in a relatively short timeframe by tuning out the noisy world around him, he discounted the myth "There's just too much incoming stuff to manage," favoring the reality "Get it done right away with total focus."

- Danielle's start-to-finish attention to completing a proposal in a single day shot down the naysayer's battle cry "I'm always waiting for others to get the job done" and shone a light on the truism "I've got to work within people's schedules as best I can when I need their help or approval."

- Ed tripled his partner's accident report workload by having those previous files available; in doing so, he countered the myth "The deadlines I get are unrealistic" and demonstrated the reality "I can meet deadlines even if what I write isn't always perfect."

- By writing and delegating parts of 14 letters, Fran showed there's nothing to the myth "They give me way too much to write" and there's everything to the reality "I can break down writing tasks to manageable parts for efficiency."

So there you have the treat-and-trick, stated in reverse because the treat usually occurs to us before the trick. Again, think of a time when you achieved a minor miracle in writing anything, from a list of agenda items to a two-sentence gentle reminder to a more complex report or proposal. The mental and emotional place where you were when you won that battle is where you'll need to be when reading this book.

How This Book Can Help

Writing on deadline in hectic, distracting environments through challenging situations for demanding people requires you to have a plan, the techniques for executing it quickly, the resolve to see it through completion, and the endurance to do it all over again. This book provides those tools through the mnemonic *DASH*: *d*irection, *a*cceleration, *s*trength, and *h*ealth. (See Figure 1-3.)

Direction

You might be able to go helter-skelter into writing chores for routine cases, but not when the world around you is in chaos, or your own mind is. Getting started without knowing the road ahead runs the risk of omitting essential detail, losing control of your organization, and rambling along in a purposeless monologue. An unfocused approach to writing is akin to beginning a vacation to a culturally rich location for the first time without a plan. While you may see the most well known sites, you'd likely miss many unforgettable vistas because you left far too much up to serendipity. Doing some research and creating an itinerary not only give you a greater sense of direction, but they also get you in the vacation frame of mind before the trip actually begins, increasing your sense of adventure, fun, and anticipation.

Similarly, getting your thoughts together when writing—devising a plan—prepares you for the trip of drafting, and planning has many faces. Chapter 2 of *How to Write Fast Under Pressure* discusses how to hit the ground running when multiple writing

FIGURE 1-3: Writing with *DASH*

Quality	Chapter	Definition	Elements
Direction	2	Hitting the ground running with the end in mind.	• Knowing the road ahead • Committing idea to writing • Devising a document plan • Using idea generators
Acceleration	3	Moving quickly through any writing assignment.	• Answering the 3 Big Questions • Preferring speed to precision • Favoring quantity over quality • Getting into a writing rhythm • Maintaining momentum
Strength	4	Possessing the stamina to get the writing job done.	• Building a writer's world by addressing your environmental, mental, physical, and social domains • Employing the 5-minute, 10-minute, and 20-minute fixes to your drafts
Health	5	Maintaining productivity throughout your writing life.	• Keeping your direction, acceleration, and strength going • Stoking your creative flame • Dealing with yourself and others in meeting deadlines

tasks are due. It details seven idea generators that can jumpstart the writing process to bring that proposal, report, procedure, or policy to closure. Speedy Didi and Mopey Moe will walk you through these practices so that you can get an idea in what situations and for which personality types they best work. Each of these techniques require that you use your fingers (or voice, if you have automated speech recognition software), not just mull things over in your mind only to forget them by the time you sit down to write. These methods go a long way toward helping you write whatever is necessary, from an elaborate message to a succinct summary that captures all the essential data without belaboring the details.

Once drafting time begins, quickly answering three big questions would be a great start. Those three questions—*Where am I going?*, *When must I get there?*, and *How will I get there?*—are the same you might ask when beginning a road trip. Some trips are so short and routine that you hardly think of them. Although I wouldn't advise it, you could almost make that drive down the block to the dry cleaners and convenience store half awake. Other trips are longer, have several available routes, and require you to outthink your global positioning system when the weather is brutal or the traffic is piling up. Before you even step in the car, you should have answered all three questions, but you might change your answer to the last question, *How will I get there?*, depending on road and traffic conditions. If the delays start to build to the point that you'll be late to your destination, you may realize that you could have done a better job of answering that second question, *When must I get there?* If only you had left earlier than usual! After all, you know today is a Friday in the summer and a lot of people are making their early weekend getaways and causing huge traffic jams. Frustrated, embarrassed, and upset, you call your appointment to say you'll be late since you've been an hour in traffic and are still an hour away. The appointment tells you, "Oh, we called your office to cancel the meeting. Didn't you check your voicemail?" Looks like you didn't even answer the first question, *Where am I going?* (Nowhere and very slowly!) You knew you should have called but, you insist, you didn't have the time—as if you have the time to sit for an hour in traffic going nowhere. Writing is no different from this scenario. You need to answer these three questions to have a clear destination, a definite timeline, and a path from the first to the last word of your message. The more you have control over these matters, the faster you will write.

Acceleration

Then there's the writing itself, drafting, transferring the thoughts from your idea generator onto the screen, getting into a rhythm that keeps you going, moving to the beat of a conversation that seems so natural to you, enabling your fingers to move quickly toward the finish line. This is the substance of Chapter 3. Acceleration implies not just speed but also a consistent momentum.

Investing in a typing course or self-teaching typing skills through popular software programs would be a fine start. But with all the electronic equipment, voice software, and online resources available to writers today, why do so many of them tell me that they do whatever they can to avoid writing, cope endlessly with writer's block, struggle through drafts, and don't know when they're finished? Keep in mind that while many of these writers are inexperienced or weak in their language skills, even more are just as good as anyone else in their finished product, but they have the toughest time getting there.

Speedy Didi would have an answer to this question. She'd say that the folks who crawl through those drafts just need to learn the best way to get it done. Of course, Mopey Moe might say, "But writing is hard—that's the truth and you can't deny it!" Didi, as she always does, would have a response to Moe's mope. "Of course it's hard," she'd concede. "But is it as hard as what a plumber does when squeezing under six or seven narrow sinks a day to perform the fine-motor-skill task of securing water traps in the dark? Or as hard as the work of a carpet layer, who on his knees uses the full force of his body to hammer wood strips and staple carpet into the floor? Or as hard as a soldier who in gear half her weight goes into a dangerous area as a sitting duck for enemies bent on killing her? Gimme me a break! I'll show you what's hard!" For sure, writing is hard, but let's put it in perspective. An ounce of courage and a pound of common sense are all you'll need to employ the tips in this book.

Strength

Being strong mentally, emotionally, and physically is invaluable to good writing. We've already gotten a glimpse into Speedy Didi's tough-as-nails attitude. That's what I call strength. No one would argue that a focused writer needs to be mentally prepared and in the right emotional condition to produce words, sentences, paragraphs, and completed documents. Didi also knows that writing is a physical task. If you have a hard time imagining that, think about how efficiently you would write if your back went out, if you were contending with a high-grade fever, or if you were exhausted after hours of physical labor.

Chapter 4 discusses the habits of productive writers, not only famous ones but successful workplace writers I've had the pleasure of meeting in my travels through major corporations, small businesses, government agencies, and nonprofit organizations. The advice in this part of the book is more an exploration than a dogma. It is not a set of inflexible rules; rather, it is a collection of sensible recommendations emerging from writers who are inarguably successful at what they do. But not all of the tips will work for everyone, so you'll get plenty of ideas to try, evaluate, and choose for yourself.

The chapter is divided into two parts, "Building a Writer's World" and "Document Fixes That Will Dramatically Improve Your Writing." "Building a Writer's World" covers the domains you can control to varying degrees: environmental, mental, physical, and social. Make no mistake: Each of these domains profoundly affects your writing output. You'll see why it's a big deal to you and what you can do to maximize your writing advantages in these areas. In "Document Fixes That Will Dramatically Improve Your Writing," you will read about an approach to critiquing and fixing your own writing through what you can call the 5-Minute, 10-Minute, and 20-Minute Fixes. Once you learn them, you can decide which one to use, depending on how much time you have. The case studies and examples in this chapter relate to real work situations, and the 5-, 10-, and 20-Minute system reflects a fundamental reality—that you want to write fast and your readers want to read fast. In a mad reading dash, you would not be forgiving of certain writing mistakes and more forgiving of others; in the same vein, when in a mad writing dash, you should be quick to check for some errors and more patient about checking for others. Using this system will give you confidence in knowing that you'll get your point across coherently and address your readers' concerns even if you're not always the best wordsmith. Also, you'll gain insights into when to massage your language given the luxury of a few more minutes before sending off your message.

While much of the commentary in Chapter 4 works for me, some of it doesn't, but I know it works for others. That's why I refer to the practices of some famous writers only when I have seen their advice applied on the job by a typical employee, so you can be assured that the tip is practical.

Health

Chapter 5 centers on what it takes to keep the ball rolling, to maintain a steady flow of writing productivity. Let's call this capacity *health* because it is a long-range goal, just as our focus on our own health is for the long term. What can we do to make writing fast at work second nature to us so that we can be a key source of credibility, quality writing, and independent as well as collaborative thinking? What can we do to reduce writing-related stress that results from our own shortcomings as well as from the interruptions, demands, and miscommunications of others? What can we do to ensure that whatever good we've gained from the chapters on direction, acceleration, and strength won't be squandered down the line by our reverting to old bad habits, simple forgetfulness, misapplied practices, or missed opportunities? Just as our long-term health is dictated by the work we do and the company we keep, we'll take a deep look at the proclivities and practices of fast writers. You'll get plenty of insights into this realm by reading Chapter 5.

DASH-ing Through Your Writing Career

Once you work through *DASH*—*d*irection, *a*cceleration, *s*trength, and *h*ealth—in all its depth and discover a trick or two for your next mind-boggling proposal, report, procedure, letter, or e-mail, you'll find Chapter 6 useful in reviewing the key concepts of the book. This chapter serves two roles. First, it outlines all you've read so you can access whatever you'd like by a quick and easy read of the final chapter. Second, it suggests next steps for you to consider in writing and living with *DASH*. It's a good summary to check in with from time to time to see whether you're keeping your creative flame stoked, your fingers limber, and your enthusiasm for writing high. You may feel like Mopey Moe, but if you practice the ideas detailed in this book you'll transform into a Mercurial Moe.

One other point: This book will help not only writers looking for tips on writing fast, but it will greatly aid managers who need guidance on getting their staff to write fast. Managers should listen carefully to Speedy Didi when she speaks. She knows what she's saying, and she always says what she has to directly and respect-fully. She gets to the point (a precious skill for a manager), and she expresses concern for her staff (an essential asset for bosses and all human beings in general).

That's precisely Speedy Didi's goal in this book: to transform Mopey Moe into Mercurial Moe, lively in the task and quick to the chase, under her tutelage. Let's not waste another moment and get you started on their journey toward writing fast at work.

Direction—Hitting the Ground Running

Didi: I'll need you to write a report on that industry conference we'll
be attending the next three days.

Moe: (*blankly*) OK.

Didi: You're all right with that?

Moe: Uh . . . yeah.

Didi: (*skeptically*) We'll see.

You know what Moe is thinking, right? Why can't she do it
herself? Why me and not my teammate? Does she realize
how much time it will take to write a report about a three-
day conference? There goes Mopey Moe moping!

What Moe should be thinking about is not how hard he has it
but what he has to do. He should be thinking about this new writing
assignment that Didi has thrust on him from her perspective. What
does she want him to include in the report? What's crossing Didi's

mind are questions like: Does he know why I want that report? Does he know who will read it? Does he know what those readers will be looking for? Does he have any idea what I want in there? Does he know what's at stake for our group and the organization?

Plenty will go wrong if these two don't communicate clearly long before the conference begins about what needs to get into the report. If Moe knows at least that, he could determine what conference sessions to attend, which industry vendor booths to visit, what details to look for, and what relevance those details have to the company's business needs. Instead of whining to himself, Moe should be asking why Didi wants the report, who will be getting it, what does she want in it, how he should spin the details, when she wants it done, and where it will be discussed. Those thoughts cannot occur to someone shrouded in doubt, resentment, or a whole host of other negative feelings.

But those questions do occur to Didi; moreover, she is keen on the fact that Moe is clueless about how to begin and what to include in the report. She sees that plane ride with Moe to the conference as the perfect time to review the contents of the report and the strategies he can employ in writing it. She knows that a sense of direction is indispensable for hitting the ground running on any writing project, so she has a bunch of what she calls "idea generators," or IGs, to redirect whatever she wants from her fertile mind to the computer screen or paper. She also knows that she is not unique in this respect and is fully aware that anybody capable of writing is also capable of using these IGs to break through writer's block.

A Vote Against Worrying

Before discussing the idea generators with Moe, Didi wants to be sure that he's in the right frame of mind to accept her advice. In other words, she needs Moe not to worry. Worrying about things beyond our control, inevitable as it may be at times, is unproductive. For example, feeling distressed about a sick child, an unemployed friend, or a relative on a foreign battlefield is entirely understandable, but our worrying alone will not make the child recover from illness or help the friend find a job or keep our family member out of harm's way. But we can comfort the child, recommend a job-seeking tip to the friend, or e-mail or phone a word of support to the soldier. On the other hand, dwelling on problems we can control seems reasonable enough; however, thinking about writing without actually writing, without actually tapping the keyboard or penciling on a piece of paper, is wasted time.

Thinking about writing, thinking to write, thinking about what you're about to write—all these are hardly better than worrying. Whether you agree with this sentiment or not is beside the point— one thing for sure is that none of them is writing. Writing does not begin until your fingers start synchronizing with what's on your mind. Everything else is wasted time if your intention is to write. The idea behind the IGs is to get your fingers synchronized with your brain so that they can start producing letters, words, sentences, paragraphs, and your ultimate message. It's all about production. Anything short of word production is preventing you from writing.

But what if you don't have the slightest idea of what to write? Then you should be researching, reading previous documents on the topic, analyzing data, and talking things over with teammates, your managers, clients, or whoever else is in the loop of the document. Preparing to write is crucial, no doubt about it. But if it's not note-taking or otherwise getting words down in front of you, it's not writing.

Understanding the Writing Process

I don't mean to say that writing is as easy as producing one perfectly crafted sentence after another in logical sequence. Writing can be hard. If it weren't, you wouldn't be reading this book for ways to make it easier. The point is a simple one: If the sentences are hard to come by, you should try writing something other than sentences. Many people erroneously think that writing well or at least writing quickly always means getting everything down in one shot, in the first draft. While accomplishing such a feat is possible in cases when the messages are routine, often our messages are directed to uninformed or unconvinced readers and laden with politically charged issues. Those are the tough ones to write—even for Didi, let alone Moe.

The problems with thinking that good writing does not require rewriting are legion. No matter how well Didi writes, the chances are strong that her manager will make changes (a) to suit his style to the given situation, (b) to add relevant detail that only he knows, (c) to change the structure to either strengthen or soften the forcefulness of the message depending on who's reading it, or (d) simply to assert his authority as Didi's boss. Why fret about these issues when writing the first draft? It'll face revision no matter what. Come to think of it, even if Didi were writing the draft just for herself, she might forget a thought or two and recall them after she's written the first draft, so she'll have to insert them later, in the second draft. Didi knows what all good writers know—and what Moe needs to learn: that writing is a process, which we get better at the more consciously we apply it.

Experts have described the writing process in various ways. Literally hundreds of books are available on the topic. In *The Business Writer's Handbook*, Gerald J. Alred, Charles T. Brusaw, and Walter E. Oliu refer to the writing process as "five steps to successful writing," namely, preparation, research, organization, writing a draft, and revision. *English Composition and Grammar*, by John E. Warriner, details the writing process as prewriting, writing a first draft, evaluating, revising, proofreading, and writing the final version. In the article "Hand, Eye, Brain: Some Basics in the Writing Process," rhetorician Janet Emig lists the writing process steps as prewriting, writing, and revision; in fact, she suggested that the writing process is so organic that it varies according to the chronological, experiential, and developmental levels of the writer. Donald Murray, another writing process researcher, wrote in the essay, "Internal Revision: A Process of Discovery," that writing comprises prevision, vision, and revision to account for all moments of reflecting on writing from unconscious to conscious activities. In my book *The Art of On-the-Job Writing*, I describe the writing process in the workplace as far less complicated, as boiling down to three basic steps: planning, when brainstorming and organizing ideas; drafting, when composing the rough copy for review; and quality controlling, when revising, editing, and proofreading the draft.

But if writing fast is all that matters, then it might make sense to see writing as occurring in two alternating phases: the creative and the critical. No matter what we call the steps of the writing process, and regardless of whether we are planning, preparing, researching, organizing, drafting, rewriting, revising, editing, or proofreading, our creative and critical sides are always struggling for our attention. What's important to remember here is not the steps so much as what's going on in our mind at any moment of the writing process. No matter whose writing process we subscribe to—my writing-process theory or any other theorist's—we need to remember that our creative and critical sides are always at tension when writing, and our job is to make sure that their warring nature doesn't get the best of us. The problem in writing efficiently occurs when the creative and the critical are at odds with each other; the solution is to get them in harmony with each other. We should think of them not as exclusive but as interdependent. After all, we can't write with half a brain, can we? Think of Sigmund Freud's conflicting id and superego, which need the modifying ego, or the Tao's *yin* and *yang*, which are corrected by the Middle Way. You can't have one without the other, so you might as well find ways of balancing both.

Let's relate this idea to the writing process by taking more than a superficial look at what's happening in our brain when we are composing. Before we begin writing sentences, we may quickly generate ideas (a creative task), but we're also sorting out those ideas by changing, adding, deleting, or moving them (a critical task). Similarly, when drafting, we are on a trip of pure speed and volume (a creative task), but we have our plan square in our mind and seek some sort of uniformity (a critical task) so that we don't stray too far from the point. For instance, when writing a status report on an office renovation project, we aren't going to start writing about our favorite football team's chances of winning the Super Bowl or about the new baked ziti recipe that Aunt Anna gave us. Even when revising, editing, and proofreading, which are primarily critical tasks, we employ quite a bit of creativity in shaping a more powerful opening or closing, rephrasing an awkward sentence, reconsidering an imprecise word, and choosing a more effective one. So it's not all as cut-and-dried as we might think. The perfectionist in us (critical) prevents us from moving forward during the first draft (creative), while the desire to choose an engaging phrase (creative) can be stifled by a slavish adherence to boilerplate, or standard, text (critical). We've got to take charge by knowing what's going on in our heads when we're hanging around with that opening sentence. Then we can deal with how much time we can give it without tweaking it endlessly and needlessly so that we can move on to the next word, sentence, paragraph, and message. Figure 2-1 shows how our creative and critical sides are always at work when writing.

Here is a brief look at how the creative and the critical phases can pop up at any given time during the writing process.

FIGURE 2-1: Understanding the Writing Process

Right Brain: The "Creative" Phase
1. Brainstorming ideas
3. Creating a rough draft
5. Reflecting from the reader's viewpoint
8. Choosing words and syntax inventively

Writing for yourself!

Writing for your readers!

Left Brain: The Critical Phase
2. Organizing ideas
4. Sticking to the plan while drafting
6. Reorganizing paragraphs
7. Critiquing sentence structure
9. Detecting overlooked errors

Planning

When planning, we quickly brainstorm and organize ideas. We're not yet writing sentences; instead, we might be listing ideas vertically, similar to a shopping list. For instance, say you were writing an overview of a training program you were coordinating for your staff. You might create a list, at first in no particular order:

> budget

> schedule

> facility

> travel

> security needs

> computer needs

> training manuals

> participants

> contacts

Or you might create the points by drawing pictures to represent ideas, such as $ for budget, ☺ for schedule, 🏠 for facility, ✈ for travel, 🔒 for security, 🖥 for computers, ☐ for manuals, ✝ for participants, and ☎ for contacts—whatever it takes to capture ideas rapidly.

But if you take that listing in super-slow motion, you might realize that you weren't only creatively listing; you might have been critiquing your list as you went along, changing the order of ideas, stopping to count how many ideas you have, even glancing at the list for a moment and instantly realizing that you're going off track or staying right on it. Come to think of it, the decision to plan a message can be seen as a creative or a critical judgment. The point here is to get both sides of your brain in harmony. Speed surely matters when planning a message because you don't want to forget anything that you might use in the drafting step, so you have two choices here, each of which works depending on your inclination:

> ‣ Brainstorm first and organize second.

> ‣ Brainstorm and organize interchangeably.

Drafting

Assuming you have a plan or you get started without a written plan because you have one in your head, you once again are balancing your creative right brain and your critical left brain. It's one thing to say that you're composing a draft with little regard for quality of structure and expressiveness, knowing that you'll have the time to fix those issues later. It's another thing to actually separate the two tasks. You could think of drafting as driving an SUV (my acronym for *speed, uniformity,* and *volume*):

> ‣ *Speed.* Keep those fingers moving without concern for errors along the way to ensure you get your ideas into sentence form. That steady rhythm you achieve helps create the momentum toward the final sentence. This drive toward creating words and sentences, however, may be counterbalanced by the critical decision to cut-and-paste some content from a previous document to make you get to the end quicker.

> ‣ *Uniformity.* Think creatively, not critically. If the right word doesn't come to you in the middle of a sentence, just keep going to the next sentence because you do not want to lose your train of thought. Alternatively, your moving through the draft with your plan in mind for the sake of uniformity is primarily a critical choice.

> ‣ *Volume.* Seek quantity, not quality. The more you remember, the less you'll forget; the more you have, the less you'll

need. All this seems like your creative side thinking, but all the while you have set goals in mind, goals that your critical mind has established and that you can't shake from your consciousness.

Rewriting

After getting your thoughts down in sentence form, you now turn your attention to the purposefulness, completeness, organization, tone, clarity, conciseness, and correctness of your message in the hope that your readers capture your ideas, not pointlessness, confusion, tactlessness, or sloppiness. These revising, editing, and proofreading choices you make appear to be inarguably critical chores. But are they really? Why are you at the top of your writing game sometimes and dragging along at others? Why does the right word sometimes pop into your head, apparently out of the blue, when at other times you just sit there paralyzed with an inability to move your fingers forward? In these cases, are you losing your critical edge? Definitely not! Your creative mind might be distracted by other issues. Maybe you're just too tired to come up with (or create) the right word or phrase, as if you have a systematic (or critical) procedure for such a moment. Once again, you cannot have the critical without the creative. Each needs the other to work for you.

Seven Idea Generators to Break Writer's Block

All right, enough about theory and on to some practical tips. Let's see Speedy Didi coach Mopey Moe on that flight from their office across the country to that conference as they go through seven ways to jumpstart the writing situation: *can it, set it, ask it, scoop it, chart it, post it,* and *list it.* Let's call them idea generators (IGs), to ensure that you use them, that they stick, and that they become second nature.

Idea Generator 1: Can It—Using Boilerplate

Moe: How would you like me to write a request for office supplies?

Didi: What are you ordering?

Moe: Two four-gigabyte flash drives for each of the six laptops, three staplers, a box of staples, three tape dispensers, a box of cellophane tape, and assorted color pens.

Didi: How do you think?

Moe: I'm not sure. That's why I'm asking you.

Didi: This is a routine order.

Moe: Yeah.

Didi: So use routine language. Don't reinvent the wheel.

Moe should not even have to ask about writing such a routine request; instead, he should just use canned language, or boilerplate. He has written such requests a thousand times in his previous job, so why shouldn't the following message work:

> Bob,
>
> The Systems Group requests the following supplies:
>
> - 12 4-gigabyte flash drives
> - 3 automatic staplers
> - 1 box of 10,000 staples

> - 3 cellophane tape dispensers
> - 48 rolls of ½"cellophane tape
> - 24 assorted color pens
>
> Please let us know if we cannot receive any of these items within two weeks.
>
> Thanks,
>
> Moe

Nothing exciting about that e-mail, but it works. Moe should *can* that one, using it again and again for the same basic request. Besides the obvious "Attached is" and "As you requested," scores of situations pop up at work all the time when you can use canned language. Create a library of openings and corresponding closings for your most common writing situations, as suggested in Figure 2-2. This idea generator is a good way of turning a blank screen into meaningful words related to your message—provided that you do not use them senselessly. When the situation calls for a compelling opening or a break from the routine, you can still use canned language, but reread your draft for appropriateness of style before pressing the send button!

Idea Generator 2: Set It—Creating Basic Templates

Moe: What do you want me to put in this procedure?

Didi: Hmm. Good question.

Moe: I mean, I know I've got to put in the steps to complete it.

Didi: Let's see.

Moe: But I want to know what else.

FIGURE 2-2: Using Canned Language

Document	Opening	Closing
Incident Investigation	This report summarizes the accident this morning when the Pillbox, Inc., truck damaged the overhead gate at Dock 3.	We will submit the repair bill to Pillbox for reimbursement and extend by 12 inches all loading dock bumpers on Friday morning.
Lab Analysis	The R&D Group submits its analysis of the enzymes found in the Bound Corporation's tetromimeosis sampling.	Further analysis of in-stock and future tetromimeosis samples from Bound Corporation and Gauge, Inc., is warranted.
Meeting Summary	Below are the minutes of the Quality Assurance Team's meeting on July 2.	The Quality Assurance Team will meet again on July 16 in the conference room.
Procedure	The following are instructions for operating and maintaining the SeeMeNow Model 8185 photocopier.	If you need operating or maintenance information not noted in this procedure, go to www.seemenow.com/8185.
Proposal	The A Team recommends the purchase of an *InYourHand* smartphone for each project manager.	For more information, go to www.InYourHand.biz. With your approval, we will process the required requisition.
Request	Please provide the following information.	We'd appreciate your prompt response.
Response to Request	Here is the information you requested.	Please let me know if you need further information.
Staff Recommendation	I strongly recommend Julian Berrios as your product manager because his diligence, creativity, and loyalty would contribute significantly to meeting your departmental objectives.	I am confident that your department will be a better one for selecting Julian, and I would be pleased to answer any questions you might have about his exceptional qualifications.
Status Report	Here is the update on the Main Street power line rerouting project.	We will issue our completion report on August 21 after installing final line testing.

Didi: Like what?

Moe: I dunno.

Didi: What else would users need to know?

Moe: What to do if the procedure doesn't work for them.

Didi: Yes, the *troubleshooting*. Anything else?

Moe. I dunno. Maybe a listing of people allowed to perform the procedure.

Didi: Yes, the *authorized user*. Is that it?

Moe: I dunno. Like if they need anything before they get started?

Didi: Yes, the *materials* needed.

Moe. I think that's it. Thanks.

Didi: Glad to help.

If this dialogue weren't so sad, it would be funny. Mopey Moe knows the answers to his questions, asserts to his boss only that he doesn't know, and truly believes that the ideas were his boss's and not his own. This behavior is not as uncommon as you might think. We are all aware of pompous fools who take credit for every idea ever imagined, but we are less conscious of the opposite type, the one who thinks every idea is brilliant and novel, as if the idea had never occurred to him. Whenever we hear someone say something that sounds profound, we are often, in fact, allowing that someone to summarize for us what we already intuitively know. For instance, suppose you have already read something in this book so new to you that you have had a eureka moment, an insight that you believe did not exist in your experience. While I might like to take credit for that insight, the truth is that you already have been thinking about the issue for it to make sense to you. So if you think, let's say, that my discussion earlier in this chapter about your creative and critical sides is a novel way of looking at writing, then think again. The chances are that all you've done is check what I've written against the last few messages you've written. It makes sense in terms of what your experience tells you.

At least Mopey Moe does deserve credit for one thing. Rather than doing nothing, he immediately bounces ideas off Speedy Didi about which elements to include. But, to make sure that Moe doesn't always have to come to her so that he can be more confident when writing, Didi recommends that he create templates of the most common writing situations that occur on the job. Figure 2-3 gives a list of 16 common documents composed by corporate writers, ranging from the administrative to the technical.

We do not always need to include all the elements in our documents, and quite often the listed elements are not enough for our readers. Say you wrote the proposal in Figure 2-4. Depending on who your readers are, the standard (Our project plan lists October 1 as the completion date for Phase 1) may be too obvious to include, the cause (Once Tom reassigned Jane to R&D on September 9, we were able to complete only three tests a week) may be politically insensitive, and the next step (Please let me know how to proceed during our next project meeting) may be too weak. In addition, the paragraphing may change if the proposal gets lengthier. You may have to separate the impact from the problem. But at least the template gives you a starting point to work from.

Idea Generator 3: Ask It—Using the 5W & H

Didi: (*sees Moe staring blankly at his laptop*) Whom are you writing to?

Moe: Our staff.

Didi: About what?

(*text continues on page 46*)

FIGURE 2-3: Setting Templates in Motion

Document	Description	Contents
Internal Proposal	Proposal or justification to management to accept a change in a work scope, head count, project cost, or production timeline	1. problem 2. history 3. impact 4. cause 5. options 6. solution 7. benefit
External Proposal	Sales proposal to a client describing a proposed business engagement	1. client need 2. scope 3. schedule 4. qualifications 5. budget
Analytical Report	Analytical report on a program or project at the planning, in-progress, or completion stage	1. problem 2. history 3. method 4. results 5. conclusion
Trip Report	Report reviewing a business trip tied to the company's objectives	1. purpose 2. facility tour 3. management interview 4. documentation review 5. analysis
Course Review	Course summary report by a participant to help management assess the value of the course in advancing the company's objectives	1. objectives 2. participants 3. facilitator 4. materials 5. activities 6. assessment
Lab Report	Review of a laboratory experiment	1. problem 2. method 3. findings 4. conclusion

Document	Description	Contents
Incident Analysis	Description of a business-critical event, actions taken to manage it, and recommended short- and long-term actions to prevent its recurrence	1. problem 2. troubleshooting methodology 3. cause 4. immediate preventive measure 5. mitigation plan
Audit Report	Report noting at least three audit points from different organizational or departmental areas (e.g., management, documentation, fiscal controls)	1. finding 2. standard 3. observation 4. cause 5. impact 6. conclusion 7. recommendation 8. benefit
Meeting Summary	Description of the key points and action items discussed at a staff meeting	1. meeting purpose, attendees 2. item 1, discussion, action, owner 3. item 2, discussion, action, owner 4. next meeting
Policy	Description of a new policy and the procedure for executing it	1. rationale for policy 2. description of procedure 3. troubleshooting
Procedure	Step-by-step instructional document intended for end users	1. procedure purpose 2. authorized user 3. required tools 4. precautions 5. numbered steps 6. troubleshooting
Self-appraisal	Employee self-evaluation for periodic managerial review describing how an employee's accomplishments align with the company's objectives and help the business	1. personal objectives for period 2. accomplishments, objective 1 3. accomplishments, objective 2 4. new personal objectives 5. plan for achieving objectives

FIGURE 2-3: Setting Templates in Motion (continued)

Document	Description	Contents
Staff Appraisal	Manager's evaluation of a subordinate	1. personal objectives for period 2. accomplishment, objective 1 3. accomplishment, objective 2 4. area for improvement 1 5. area for improvement 2 6. action plan for next period
Staff Recommendation	Staff endorsement to another manager within the company or to another employer	1. relationship 2. aptitude 3. attitude 4. aspirations
Disciplinary Action	Reprimand of a staff member for violating company policy	1. infraction 2. history 3. policy 4. expectations 5. consequences
Job Application	Personal statement in application for a position	1. company objectives 2. qualifications fit 3. anticipated results

Moe: The mitigation plan for Client XYZ's complaint about slow service.

Didi: Why?

Moe: Because we want to provide great service.

Didi: When do we have the problem?

Moe: Only when responding to inquiries.

Didi: Where does the problem occur most?

Moe: When our managers are in remote locations for extended periods.

Didi: How will you mitigate the problem?

Moe: I've got this three-part procedure in my head: First, the sales

FIGURE 2-4: Proposal Template

1. Summary	Asking R&D to reassign Jane to Project Now would recover some production time lost since she left the project.[1]
	Problem
2. Problem 3. Standard 4. Finding 5. Impact	Project Now is running behind schedule.[2] Our project plan lists October 1 as the completion date for Phase 1,[3] but we have seven tests to run before we can move to Phase 2.[4] At this rate, we will not complete the project until December 14, two weeks past the projected completion date.[5]
6. History 7. Cause	We planned the timeline for this project assuming three analysts would conduct the Phase 1 tests.[6] Once Tom reassigned Jane to R&D on September 9, we were able to complete only three tests a week.[7]
	Options
8. Method	I've estimated the time needed to complete the final seven tests and discussed with the remaining analysts three options to get to within a week of the deadline:[8]
9. Options	1. *Allow overtime.* Because of the painstaking level of testing, the extended working hours may compromise quality. 2. *Assign me to the testing team.* In this scenario, I would have to suspend my supervisory responsibilities. 3. *Reassign Jane.* This option would help us regain continuity and ensure sufficient coverage without sacrificing quality or supervision.[9]
	Recommendation
10. Solution 11. Benefit	Returning Jane is our best option[10] to gain at least a week of lost time.[11]
12. Next Step	Please let me know how to proceed during our next project meeting.[12]

staff copies me when they respond to any client request. Then I decide whether to leave the issue for the salesperson, handle it myself, or dispatch it to the help desk—whoever can get it done the fastest. Finally, regardless of the choice, I drop a message to the client with the choice, copying the salesperson and whoever is handling the situation.

Didi: That's why I hired you.

Moe: Yeah, yeah. I can talk this stuff, but I can't write it.

Didi: You just did.

When planning the direction you want your message to take, how many ways are there for conducting a question-and-answer session? Countless! Asking and answering self-imposed questions before drafting, you'll see your fingers dance across the page. Just reflecting on the old but reliable 5W&H (*who*, *what*, *why*, *when*, *where*, *how*), not necessarily in any particular order, you'll see a flood of ideas pouring in. Take another look at Didi's questions in that last dialogue. She actually walked Moe through the 5W&H!

Those questions work in all sorts of situations. Here's an example of a meeting announcement:

> *Why* are we meeting?
>
> *When* will we meet?
>
> *Where* will we meet?
>
> *Who* should attend?
>
> *What* will we discuss?
>
> *How* should they prepare for the meeting?

And here's an incident report:

> *What* happened?
>
> *Who* was involved or affected?
>
> *When* did it happen?
>
> *Where* did it happen?
>
> *What* was the impact of the incident?
>
> *How* was it resolved or will it be resolved?

You can work through all 16 of the templates in Figure 2-3 to see for yourself how the 5W&H will get your writing going in the right direction. Of course, you can ask so many other questions about your message rather than a single *who, what, why, when, where,* or *how*. Sometimes it takes two *what's* or four *why's* or six *how's* or no *when's* at all. Use the judgment of the only person you can really trust: yourself.

Idea Generator 4: Scoop It—Stating the Purpose

Moe: I need a writing class.

Didi: Why would I want to approve that?

Moe: Because if I communicate as powerfully in writing as I do in speaking, our team would look more professional.

Didi: Bingo!

Chances are that Moe once again missed the wisdom of his brief chat introducing the need for some writing training. In those two sentences, he clearly stated the two most important ideas if he'd have to write a justification:

> *What he wants*. His boss should approve a writing class for him.

> *Why the person he wants it from should want it, too*. He'll come across as powerfully in writing as he does in speech, thereby making the team look more professional.

When journalists are the first to get their hands on a story, they say that they've scooped the competition. Moe's statement is a sort of scoop, too. In those mere 24 words, which in their finished written form would be reduced to 22 words ("A writing class would help me communicate as powerfully in writing as I do in speaking, making our team look more professional"), he's setting up Didi with seven propositions, and in doing so he is helping her scoop him:

1. He is not as good a writer as he thinks he can be.

2. He needs a writing class.

3. He speaks powerfully.

4. Writing is in some way akin to speaking.

5. A writing class will help him write powerfully.

6. The team could be more professional than it is.

7. His writing powerfully will help the team look more professional.

Better than letting Didi scoop him, Moe is scooping himself. By starting with these propositions in a condensed statement, he knows the direction his justification memo will take. He'll surely have to discuss his weak points in writing, what type of course would help him write more powerfully, best practices he shows in speaking that he does not show in writing, how writing powerfully would improve the professionalism of the team, and so on. He has plenty to go on.

The simple beauty of his two sentences is this: He merged purpose and audience, the two keys to a direct style that most businesses demand from their staff. You can call the purpose part of the sentence the *what's-in-it-for-me* and the audience-benefit part of the sentence the *what's-in-it-for-you*. Figure 2-5 illustrates examples of the scoop.

It's important to note a few ideas about scooping. First, not all messages need a what's-in-it-for-me and what's-in-it-for-you; some messages, such as most status reports, meeting minutes, and incident reports, have neither because they are strictly for informational purposes. Also keep in mind that stating the audience benefit before the requested action is not necessary; in fact, while the what's-in-it-for-me is essential, the what's-in-it-for-you does not always need stating because it may be obvious, as in "I need

FIGURE 2-5: Examples of the Scoop

Procedure	Using the procedure detailed below *(what's in it for me)* will minimize operator error and accidents *(what's in it for you)*.
Proposal	To ensure a continuous production and a smooth transition on moving day *(what's in it for you)*, IT recommends a three-phase course of action *(what's in it for me)*.
Request	Please send the following documents *(what's in it for me)* so that we can process your application by the due date *(what's in it for you)*.
Response	I understand you are looking for ways to increase your client base *(what's in it for you)*. Calling Jane Wayne, our most successful territory manager, would be beneficial to that end *(what's in it for me)*.

the key to my office so I can get in and do my job for you.'' (Those last 11 words are useless and possibly sarcastic.) In general, however, stating the what's-in-it-for-you first is more deferential to the reader, while stating the what's-in-it-for-me first is more assertive. No matter how you start the message, you are scooping the story for the reader, summarizing it up front as a promise to deliver. We often make assertions, denials, and promises in writing without completely delivering on them. By taking what he says literally, Moe can let the sentence guide him through the draft, deciding what content stays and what leaves by checking it against the scoop. One final word of advice: Don't make the scoop so mechanical to the point of triteness. This sentence is too important to include without writing it with authority and conviction.

Idea Generator 5: Chart It—Mapping Your Ideas

> Moe: Sometimes issues are so complicated that to make them real I see them as pictures, not words.

> Didi: Then draw your plan!

> Moe: Huh?

Didi: If you think the limitations of language are getting in your way, why use language? Use pictures!

Much research has been done on this topic. Consultants like Tony and Barry Buzan (*The Mind Map Book*) and Joyce Wycoff (*Mindmapping*) argue that humans imagine ideas in pictures, not words, so thinking in words restricts imaginative thinking. While experience tells me and many others that this claim is not always the case, why argue with the idea generator itself? Drawing picture diagrams may very well be a better way to capture ideas quickly in some situations. Figure 2-6 shows a variation as old as mindmapping, what I call "charting," which you can do on either a piece of paper or a computer. Charting may work better for writers whose artistic powers exceed their ability to use words.

In the example, an administrative assistant has to cull the results of 12 employee survey questions. First, she groups them into four categories: Management, Training, Career, and Benefits. Then she decides to order them based on frequency of employee response. With this simple plan before her, she now has a reporting structure for her draft.

Idea Generator 6: Post It—Creating Moveable Notes

Didi: You ran a great meeting yesterday.

Moe: Thanks.

Didi: I liked how you posted everyone's ideas on the whiteboard.

Moe: Yeah.

Didi: First you listed everything randomly, then you rearranged them. You can use post-its the same way to get your thoughts together when writing.

Moe: Really?

FIGURE 2-6: Charting It—Getting from Here to There

Issues in Order of Most Frequent Response

1. Health insurance choices
2. Condensed workweek
3. Virtual office
4. Promotional opportunities

5. Tuition reimbursement
6. Relocation requirements
7. Distance education
8. Company expansion plans

9. In-house training programs
10. Frequent management briefings
11. Industry trends
12. Clear communication

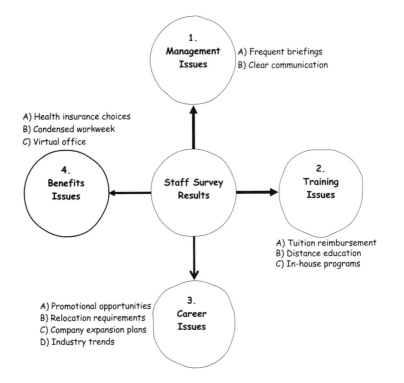

Here's a technique you may find useful if your computer is not around but a pack of post-its or index cards is. With your topic in mind, get all your thoughts down, one idea per post-it, then rearrange them in groups, say one group per paragraph. While grouping ideas, you will probably find yourself adding and deleting ideas based on your structure and what you think your readers need to know. In Figure 2-7, a building contractor sits in his SUV at 10:30

FIGURE 2-7: Posting

time frame	shower door	tile wall & floor	roof replacement
back deck	house access	cost	insurance
labor only option	payment terms	qualifications	references

1. Exterior

roof replacement

back deck

2. Interior

shower door

tile wall & floor

3. Requirements

time frame

cost

payment terms

house access

4. Requested Info

labor only option

insurance

qualifications

references

A.M. immediately after a sales visit to a prospective client. He still has two other client appointments, so he wants to make sure that when he gets to the office he can immediately crank out three diverse proposals. First, he scatters a few post-its on his notebook and jots notes from the meeting in no particular order. Then he arranges them under four categories in the order in which he will address them in his proposal. When he gets into the office at 4:00 P.M., he'll be ready to rip through this proposal.

Idea Generator 7: List It—Outlining Key Points

Moe: So what about the conference report?

Didi: It's got to be as comprehensive as possible because it'll go to the CEO's office, Finance, Human Resources, Information Technology, Production, Marketing, and Research and Development.

Moe: I know I've got to write a summary of each session and its relevance to our business. But reporting on six 90-minute sessions over two days is brutal.

Didi: Just create bullet lists of everything you hear at each session and then dress them up in sentences. Be sure to arrange the sessions and the key points from each not in chronological order but in order of importance, from most-to-least important.

These words of advice from Didi give Moe a plan for writing his document and a purpose for listening at the conference. Figure 2-8 has two parts, the first showing how he experienced the conference (as if anyone from the Executive Office, Finance, Human Resources, Information Technology, Production, Marketing, and Research and Development cares!) and the second reshaped based on what he thinks will work best for his readers. For Part 1, he does little more than list information pouring into his head; in Part 2, he is making sense of the information, deciding what goes and what stays, what's most important, what needs a conclusion before a reason and vice versa. He may be wrong in some of his decisions, but who cares? At least he can start drafting with all that content and have a working copy in front of Didi for her review before she kicks it upstairs to management.

Listing is helpful to writers coping with information overload because they start directly on the computer, wasting no time doodling or cogitating. In fact, of the seven techniques, only charting and posting are done off-screen, one of the main reasons to use them less because any time away from the computer when writing assignments are due tends to be wasted time. Nevertheless, I often hear people tell me that the lifeless flat screen before them inhibits their creative thinking. If that's so, you should try charting or posting on paper.

The Three Big Questions

After creating such a well-organized list, Moe has no reason to mope. He should feel pretty good about writing that draft. He

FIGURE 2-8: Listing

PART 1: Moe lists ideas as they occur to him during the workshop sessions he attends.

Session 1: Widgetry Industry Trends
  1. ISO certification changes
  2. Outsourcing

Session 2: Creating a Need in Overseas Widget Markets
  1. Latin America—economic standards
  2. Southeast Asia—cultural differences
  3. Middle East—political stability

Session 3: New Safeguards by the National Widgetry Regulatory Commission
  1. Audit expectations
  2. Retooling costs
  3. Management accountability
  4. Safety engineering

Session 4: Moving from Just-in-Time Widget Inventorying
  1. More orders, smaller shipments
  2. New demands on warehousing

Session 5: Research and Development: Connecting the Widget Industry with the University
  1. Shrinking talent supply
  2. Prohibitive in-house R&D costs
  3. Greater need for production and warehousing space
  4. Federal and state tax advantages to university outreach

Session 6: The Diminishing Widget Supplier Base
  1. India shifting from widgets to IT
  2. Indonesia price hikes
  3. Possible solution: Persuade China to retool
  4. Possible solution: Upgrade and partner with ill-equipped African suppliers

PART 2: Moe reorganizes the ideas, deleting and adding as he goes along, according to what he believes to be the points of greatest interest to his readers. The deleted items are crossed out and the added items appear in a different font.

~~Session 6:~~ The Diminishing Widget Supplier Base
1. India shifting from widgets to IT
2. Indonesia price hikes
3. ~~Possible solution: Persuade China to retool~~
4. ~~Possible solution: Upgrade and partner with ill-equipped African suppliers~~
- Reasons that China and Africa are not options for us
- Suggestion: Create an in-house taskforce to study the situation

~~Session 3:~~ New Safeguards by the National Widgetry Regulatory Commission
- Suggestion: 3. Management accountability and 4. Safety engineering will be needed because of 1. Audit expectations and 2. Retooling costs

~~Session 4:~~ Moving from Just-in-Time Widget Inventorying
1. More orders, smaller shipments result in 2. New demands on warehousing
- Suggestion: Rethink how we use space

~~Session 1:~~ Widgetry Industry Trends
- Suggestion: Hire a consulting engineer to develop ISO conversion plan
1. ISO certification changes—huge impact on our industry standing

~~Session 5:~~ Research and Development: Connecting the Widget Industry with the University
- Suggestion: may be a great recruiting mechanism because of 1. Shrinking talent supply
4. Federal and state tax advantages to university outreach
2. ~~Prohibitive in-house R&D costs~~
3. ~~Greater need for production and warehousing space~~

~~Session 2:~~ Creating a Need in Overseas Widget Markets Just an Overview
1. Latin America—economic standards, 2. Southeast Asia—cultural differences, 3. Middle East—political stability

has that sense of direction he so craves to power him through the document. He is at the point where he might very well have the answers to the Three Big Questions every polished writer should have before taking on a writing assignment: *Where am I going?*, *When must I get there?*, and *How will I get there?* Writing is a journey, a drive to work, a trip to the mall, a leisurely interstate tour accompanied by your favorite music. Sure, it can be bumpy at times, but remembering the answers to the Three Big Questions will keep you alert at the wheel. Whenever your back is against the wall and you feel you just can't get a required writing task done, ask them.

1. **Where am I going?** Answering this question demands a purpose statement and a specific audience. Examples include:

> ‣ I am going to my manager with a proposal for a laptop.

> ‣ I am going to the entire company with a new corporate security policy.

> ‣ I am going to my client with an action plan for an efficient production process.

2. **When must I get there?** Answering this question locks you into a no-excuse and no-nonsense commitment to finishing the writing task *at a specific time*. You never want to accept your readers' deadline—you want to beat them by a mile! Examples:

> ‣ If my manager expects the proposal by Thursday, I'll be done by Wednesday.

> ‣ If the company needs the policy by tomorrow morning, I'll be done before lunch today.

> ‣ If my client wants the action plan in an hour, I'll be done 15 minutes after I get off the phone with him.

3. **How will I get there?** If answering the first two questions revs you up with a sense of urgency, purpose, focus, and drive, then answering this last question requires a straightforward attack of the supporting details, which you can gather through any of the seven idea generators we've discussed. Examples:

> ‣ For the laptop proposal to my manager, I need to mention the options, cost, benefits, etc.

> ‣ For the policy to the entire company, I need the policy description, its effective date, the staff affected, the reason for the policy, etc.

> ‣ For the client action plan, I need the plan benefit, plan description, troubleshooting process, etc.

Now that we've covered the writing process, it would be a good idea to remember the Three Big Questions at every step of the process: when generating ideas during planning, when firing off a rough copy while drafting, or when revising, editing, and proofreading at the rewriting step. The Three Big Questions lock you in the *writing zone* by keeping your eyes on the "small picture," the purpose of your message and your audience's interests and concerns. Your mind can now be led by the true north that your answers to the Three Big Questions give you. Without knowing the answers to these questions, you'd be lucky to know the answer to the most basic of questions: Who am I? Where am I? Why am I here? And if you can't answer these simple questions, you are truly lost. By answering the Three Big Questions, then, you can infer that you are self-possessed, confident, and fast.

A Brief Note on Automatic Speech Recognition Software

I keep meeting more people extolling the virtues of their automatic speech recognition (ASR) programs, claiming it has reduced their fear of writing and increased their writing output. Employees who tell me that they can't type well are especially appreciative of ASR. I've also heard some parents, many of learning-disabled children, say that their children possesses adequate reading comprehension skills and can speak reasonably well about what they've read or can argue a point fluently but have only limited success when processing ideas in writing. ASR may be a big help to them.

Those claims are impossible for me to counter because we don't argue against our own evidence. If someone says she writes faster and better using ASR, who would know better than she, and who am I to argue with her? If that's what works for you, keep using it. Having played with ASR myself, I can see why people enjoy using it and find it relatively fast. It definitely moves faster than my fingers, as is the case for most everyone, and if you're using ASR for the first time you will be impressed with its accuracy.

Yet I find the ASR miscues annoying, even though they appear less often than those from unskilled typists who fat-finger the keyboard with doubled, inaccurate characters. More important, I've grown accustomed to the connection between the brain and the fingers. I also find myself writing, as many people do, at times and in places that might not lend themselves to using ASR, such as meetings when I'm taking notes and public conveyances where I'm free of office distractions and more likely to write voluminously.

In any event, this book is about encouraging you to try whatever available breakthrough technique works for you. If you've heard that ASR is worth trying, then find out for yourself. Pursue all options, deciding what's best for you based on how the idea generator picks up your word processing speed.

3

Acceleration—Writing on the Fly

Moe: I feel like I'm always racing against the clock!

Didi: You may feel that way. But you set the clock you race against.

Let's face it: No one can make you go faster than you can go—no one except yourself. If you've read Chapter 2 while carefully reflecting on the kind of writing you do at work, then you've had a chance to decide which idea generator for breaking writer's block might work best for you. You now have a few approaches to the writing situation, whether you're parked in your car, sitting in a coffee shop, hammering away at the keyboard at your desk, or lounging on a couch at home or a chaise on the beach. Chapter 2 was all about the need to have a clear course of action to give you a sense of direction that will guide you from start to finish. Planning the rough draft is that important.

But do we always need to plan? Obviously not. You plan drafts to save time, not waste it. If you're stuck staring at the screen without producing words, then plan; if you can skip planning and write a reasonably good first draft, then do it.

The Three Varying Levels of Writing Complexity at Work

We need to make the writing process work for us by not subjecting basic writing tasks, such as ordinary requests and responses, to unnecessary steps. On the other hand, we shouldn't reduce longer, more challenging tasks to simple steps that are insufficient to account for the scope of the project. The brain is quicker than the hand, so we need to break through anything that gets in the way of our fingers moving across the keyboard, typing words, maybe not the best words, choicest phrases, or powerful images but at least thoughts intelligible enough to get our point across, if only for now to ourselves, the writer. The readers can wait until we rewrite. Using the whole process, then, is not always essential. Our writing at work generally falls into three situations, the *free*, the *formulaic*, and the *fresh*, and depending on which category we find ourselves writing in, we should make the process work for us.

We're in free mode when writing simple messages that come to us easily, almost as easily as speaking with a friend. Think of those quick e-mails: *Please send the quarterly sales report . . . Would you know how to access the vendor database? . . . Below is the agenda of our next meeting . . . Here are the procedures for using and troubleshooting the XYZ.* When writing these no-brainer messages, we have no need for planning or, for that matter, revising, editing, and proofreading. All we do is draft.

Formulaic writing is far more challenging because of its official nature, but it is easy in the sense that we know the details, structure, and format expected of us. When completing an incident investigation, for instance, the police officer, quality assurance manager, or technical analyst knows to give a chronological accounting of what incident happened, what was done to investigate it, what its impact was, what its causes were, what was done to correct it, and what can be done to prevent its recurrence. In writing a meeting summary, the administrative assistant or other staff correspondent knows to include the meeting attendees, the purpose of the meeting, the points discussed, the action item, and the staff responsible for fulfilling them. There are many more formulaic documents, such as status reports, executive summaries, staff appraisals, product evaluations, product specifications, and lab analyses, to name a few. So formulaic are these documents that many organizations set up templates in which the writer just needs to fill in the boxes. If this is the case, then the planning step, in which we create a rough structure for the draft, is unnecessary because the structure has already been created. All we have to do is draft what we need to include and probably do some editing and proofreading because many different readers will receive the message and we will want it to look as good as we can make it. While formulaic messages are more challenging to compose than free messages, at least we begin them knowing what details we need for them.

Fresh writing, on the other hand, demands the most of us. In these moments, we might not immediately know the main point or the intended readers; as a result, we go into the drafting situation grasping for the right details, structure, or style. For this reason, we have to create a plan before drafting because our brain is either overloaded with ideas or a complete blank, or our heart is either full of fury or just not into it. Devising a plan always helps in these situations so that we can jump into drafting mode on just the right note and temperament. In effect, we plan only when we need to break through writer's block, as Figure 3-1 illustrates. Once you

FIGURE 3-1: Using the Writing Process Wisely

Situation	1. Planning	2. Drafting	3. Rewriting
1. Free		✓	
2. Formulaic		✓	✓
3. Fresh	✓	✓	✓

know you're in a fresh writing situation, you can turn to one or more or a combination of the seven idea generators for breaking writer's block. That kind of thinking will get your creative juices flowing, energy level accelerated, and sense of direction on track.

Keep in mind that the examples I've used for the free, formulaic, and fresh types of writing are entirely subjective. What may be formulaic for me may be fresh for you, and what may be fresh for me may be free for you. When you start working for a new company, for instance, virtually every document is a challenging one; therefore, the complexity level increases, requiring more steps of the writing process. The trick is to make many of the documents you write formulaic so that you can always use previously written messages to set the framework or can the language, thereby increasing your speed. (See the section on idea generators in Chapter 2, setting it and canning it.)

Setting the Clock: The Four Ds of Managing Writing Tasks

Let's return to Didi's remark to Moe at the top of this chapter: "You set the clock you race against." She's saying this because she's hearing from Moe an extremely negative, self-defeating message. By moaning, "I feel like I'm always racing against the clock!" he is going into the writing task in the belief that he will fail. Even an uncertain "How can I get this done on time?" would have made Didi happier. As a manager, she can answer Moe's questions, but she'll weary soon enough of being a psychotherapist. What does Moe expect Didi to say in response to his lament? "Why do you feel that way? . . . How long have you been feeling that way? . . . How do you know for sure? . . . Would you like some anti-anxiety medication?" If Moe had thought for a moment how he would react if a subordinate had said to him what he had said to Didi, he would never have uttered it himself. It amounts to stonewalling the work at hand.

Moe could have gotten started by answering the Three Big Questions:

1. **Where am I going?** To a completed rough draft of the six-session conference report.

2. **When will I get there?** It's 9:00 A.M. now, so I'll aim for 10:30 A.M. for Didi to get a chance to review it with comments. Then I'll leave 4:00 P.M. to 5:00 P.M. open to make any revisions for final submission tomorrow at 8:30 A.M.

3. **How will I get there?** By following this outline for each session:

> Topic

> Presenters

> Theme

> Key points

> Business relevance

> Suggested management action

Then I'll cut-and-paste from the CDs provided by the speakers for Sessions 2 and 5, copy from the PowerPoint presentation notes from Session 4, and refer to my notes for Sessions 1, 3, and 6.

He's still not free and clear. This still seems like he's racing against the clock, a practice that, if it becomes his standard operating procedure, will eventually cause stress and burnout. Now he has to put on his game face, controlling *his* clock, the tick-tick-tick that he always hears in the back of his mind, whenever he has to produce work on a tight schedule. He has to tune out whatever can distract him from reaching his deadline. This, of course, is much easier said than done because he has to respond to e-mail about business-critical issues that arise each day. He has already done what he can by asking his teammate, Happy Hannah, to cover his phone messages for the next 90 minutes so that he can rush through his draft, but the e-mail is another story. No avoiding that. Only if he can dedicate his time to the writing task will he truly believe that he is running to his own clock, setting the way he will manage the next 90 minutes of his working life to produce a measureable result.

So what would Speedy Didi recommend for Moe to protect his precious time? Whenever faced with a huge volume of writing as the e-mail keeps flooding her inbox, she sets the clock by creating a mindset to help her instantly determine which e-mails she should dismiss outright or just temporarily and which e-mails are too important to ignore. In doing so, she is reckoning with the reality that diverting attention from a complex writing task to e-mail can be the number one time-killer, leading to frustration, unfocused writing, and missed deadlines. Didi puts first things first through the Four Ds—*dump, delegate, defer,* and *do*—in that order (see Figure 3-2). Here's a quick summary of the Four Ds:

1. **Dump**—always your first choice. You dump when you either delete the e-mail altogether or file it in an electronic folder.

Of course, you can't say yes to this option as often as you'd like. Many messages may have only a peripheral relationship to your work responsibilities, but peripheral is enough not to delete them. Nevertheless, thinking about dump as a first option is a timesaver that might get you to stop replying to every message that comes your way. So many are useless to the work you do; get used to treating them that way.

2. **Delegate**—a good choice if you can get away with it. The creative phase of writing—when planning and drafting from scratch—is the most time-consuming part of writing. You need to minimize distractions during this time, so asking for assistance on pressing matters that someone else can manage is a great help in saving you heaps of time.

3. **Defer**—a good choice if you just aren't ready to deal with the issue. If you lack the information to respond to a message, why waste your time staring at a blank screen? Save it for later. Caution: Don't use this option as a means of getting started when it's too late, thereby adding more pressure on yourself. When choosing the defer option, schedule your response for a specific time when you really expect to do it, rather than get into the bad habit of perpetually planning it forward in the hope that the e-mail will go away. We already dealt with that nasty habit of Mopey Moe in Chapter 1.

4. **Do**—a last resort. If you've said no to the first three options, then don't just sit there. Get started! Get that roadblock out of the way so you can continue what you're doing.

To see how you might rely on the Four Ds of managing writing tasks, put yourself in this situation: You are writing a lengthy document for your boss, a document that was due yesterday. It could

FIGURE 3-2: The Four Ds of Managing Writing Tasks

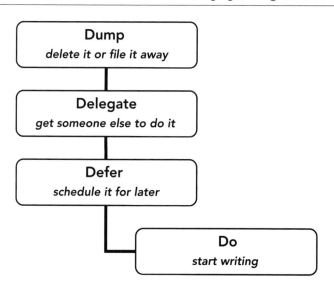

be a project description, an audit report, a client proposal, a technical specification, whatever. You are also responsible for expeditiously responding to e-mails from internal and external clients who have myriad questions, vendors who need information before delivering needed goods and services, and teammates who rely on your expertise to troubleshoot business-critical problems. While you are writing, an e-mail comes to your inbox. I'll leave the sender, situation, and content of the message up to you, but think of specific cases. To make the scenario concrete, I will use an example of four e-mails that pop into Speedy Didi's inbox while she is writing an executive summary about a complicated issue for upper management with a self-imposed deadline of 30 minutes. While your position may not allow you to make the same decisions that Didi does about each message, keep in mind her middle-management position, great value to the company, and relationships with coworkers.

E-mail 1

> **From: Boss Bobby**
>
> **Subject: New Operating Procedure**
>
> **Message: To ensure safety of all staff and security of proprietary information . . .**
>
> **Didi's Reaction: She saw this message as a dump, filing it in a folder called "Procedures" for future reference.**

This reaction may seem reckless considering that the e-mail comes from her boss and it concerns staff safety and business security. But for these very reasons, she knows that the entire organization will receive this e-mail, so her staff will read the message and discuss it with her. This e-mail continues for another 300 words or so, but all she reads is what appears in the above excerpt. Why waste her time on that message now, when she's trying to transmit a vital piece of information to management? She stops at the first of the Ds, *d*ump, without even thinking about *d*elegate, *d*efer, or *d*o.

E-mail 2

> **From: Vendor Val**
>
> **Subject: Delay in Laptop Order**
>
> **Message: I'm sorry to say that we can't ship the X388 laptops you ordered until we receive the credit**

references we requested last week. Please send this information as soon as you can along with your preferred shipping method so that we can handle your equipment needs right away.

Didi's Reaction: This one is a delegate. She forwards the message to Connie Controller with the comment: "Please handle." She also copies her subordinate, Happy Hannah.

Moving through the first D, Didi knows that she will not be able to dump the message by either deleting or simply filing it because she needs those laptops as soon as possible. She is in a position to delegate the message to a peer, Connie Controller, because she and Connie have already spoken about this issue. In fact, Connie said last week that she would send over the credit references. Perhaps Connie did and Vendor Val misplaced the information, or maybe Connie just hasn't gotten around to it yet. But Didi has a good enough relationship with Connie to know that she can get away with a two-word message, "please handle," without seeming offensive, arrogant, or even unnecessarily brusque. In addition, she has copied Happy Hannah because she and Hannah have a longstanding arrangement: Whenever Didi copies her on an e-mail, it's for Hannah's immediate resolution, unless Didi writes FYI, meaning the message is just for your information without any need for future action. (Making such arrangements with coworkers, subordinates, and managers helps greatly in speeding up the writing process. More about this in Chapter 5.) Therefore, Didi knows that she can forget about this situation because it's in good hands. By stopping at the second D, delegate, Didi never considers deferring the issue as an option, a choice that would be irresponsible considering how much she wants those laptops. It also never enters her mind to delve into the most time-consuming D—the do.

How interesting that the message in E-mail 2 from a vendor, one who should be the servant and not the superior, is more actionable for Didi than E-mail 1, the one from a manager to whom she reports. Didi is not one to have knee-jerk reactions based on the sender alone. Even though she is deciding on what to do with these messages in the blink of an eye, she is using a well-formulated system based on her experience at every moment to decide what gets done by her, what gets done by others, and what doesn't get done.

Many people tell me that delegating is never an option for them, that they are responsible for closing everything that comes their way. They are more in Happy Hannah's place, figuratively speaking, than in Speedy Didi's. I respect their claim for a number of reasons, the foremost being that they have reflected carefully on their subordinate position within their organizations, leading them to the correct conclusion that they cannot delegate a lick of their responsibilities. Additionally, they may be too powerless to delegate because of their unique talent as problem solvers, dispatchers, or support staffers, so they handle things themselves.

But I still have my doubts about such a closed-case claim; even they are delegating more than they realize. They delegate when responding "Can you handle that?" to a significant other or spouse asking about a prescription. They delegate when a friend inquires about available tickets to a show and they ask, "Can you look into it?" They delegate when doing nothing in response to a request for help their manager has broadcast to the entire group, in the hope that someone else will help to the manager's satisfaction. They delegate when, instead of writing an elaborate response to a client, they simply write, "The attached contract, Clause 6.8, will answer your question better than I can." They delegate when writing to a coworker, copied to the originator of the question, "Do you know how to answer this?" They delegate when asking their manager, "What should I say?" in response to a client e-mail. For sure, they have to choose their delegations carefully, but they still have the option to delegate, the number 2 spot of the Four Ds.

E-mail 3

> **From: Client Kelvin**
>
> **Subject: Re: Invoice 24601**
>
> **Message:** I checked out why you haven't gotten paid. You did not have a purchase order number. I know we never got one to you, but now we have one: PO081011. Would you please resubmit the invoice with the PO number? Thanks.
>
> **Didi's Reaction:** She chooses to defer this one.

There aren't many issues more important than getting paid. Didi knows that. She also knows that once she opens the e-mail, she has already spent some time with it, even if only a few seconds. One of the big principles of time management is to handle whatever you can only once and get it out of the way.

For obvious reasons, this message is not a dump, and on the surface it may seem easy enough to delegate to Happy Hannah. But it's not, because the invoice is for a specialized service not in Hannah's database, so Hannah's invoicing system will not allow her to process the unique pricing structure. Besides, by the time Didi explains everything to Hannah, she might as well have taken care of the matter herself. Since reprocessing this invoice will take three to four minutes, Didi decides these are three to four minutes she does not have right now. She'll keep this e-mail in her inbox and deal with it when she's done with her executive summary. Again, all of this decision making passes through Didi's cognitive processes in split seconds, as did E-mails 1 and 2.

E-mail 4

> From: Subordinate Mopey Moe
>
> Subject: Question about Conference Report
>
> Message: Do I need to include a Recommended Management Action for every conference topic? I'm asking because the session on "Creating a Need in Overseas Widget Markets" doesn't seem to apply to our business.
>
> Didi's Reaction: This one is a do. Didi replies with a single word: Absolutely.

At this precise moment in Didi's business life, this e-mail seems the most important for her to do immediately. First of all, dumping isn't an option because she wants that report as much as Moe wants to complete it. Plus she has no one to defer a response to because only she knows the answer to that question. (Actually, Moe himself should have known the answer to his question, which explains her intentionally terse response.) She knows she can't defer her response because Mopey Moe would sit there absolutely frozen, waiting on her word and losing valuable time. Since his question is easy enough to respond to in a single, strongly stated word, she goes for the do. Her preemptive response suggests that she doesn't want to hear any excuses, doesn't want a follow-up question—just give her what she's looking for.

Try the Four Ds technique on your inbox to see if it works for you. Chances are you already have a system that works for you sometimes but not always. Break it down to see if it works like the Four Ds. If not, it's worth a try or two to see if your efficiency at handling incoming messages improves. You also can try the Four Ds when considering writing tasks. For instance, say you want to recommend a rearrangement of workspace. Immediately call up the Four Ds:

> Is it a dump, because you'd be better off talking to the boss about it before committing it to an exhaustive written justification?

> Is it a delegate, because you can ask a coworker who is more in the know to write it for you?

> Is it a defer, because you'll have time to write it next Thursday between 2:00 and 3:00 P.M.?

> Is it a do, because this issue just can't wait and you have the time to tackle it in writing now?

Finally, the Four Ds work well in connection with the free, formulaic, and fresh levels of writing complexity. Using the same example about recommending a rearrangement of office space:

> If it's a free situation, you'll know instantly that the ease of the writing task will make you bypass the dump, delegate, and defer to get to the do. Just fire away!

> If it's a formulaic situation, you'll have a response similar to the free situation, except that you'll immediately pull

down proposal templates and set the format or use canned language to jumpstart the writing process.

> ▸ If it's a fresh writing situation, you'll tap into your time management skills, asking the Three Big Questions—*Where am I going? When must I get there?* and *How will I get there?*—and composing your message accordingly.

With the Four Ds becoming a frequently used tool in your toolbox, you have "set the clock," taking control of as much of the writing situation as you possibly can. It's now time to beat the clock and rush through a draft with your plan in hand.

Beating the Clock: Two Ways of Drafting

Didi: (*passing Moe's desk as he stares at his monitor*) What's up?

Moe: I'm writing.

Didi: Are you stuck?

Moe: No, I'm thinking.

Didi: Can't you write down what you're thinking?

Moe: It has nothing to do with what I'm writing about.

There goes another gem for Didi to remember about Moe. He claims to be writing, but he's not thinking about what he's writing. That's anything but writing, yet Moe doesn't seem to get it. Once in drafting mode, he needs to plow straight ahead, letting his fingers do an intricately linguistic dance across the keyboard. He needs to let his fingers perform the imaginative trick of doing the talking, always by managing the delicate balance between his creative and critical sides.

Now that we have gotten real by setting the clock—by setting our own timeline—let's beat the clock by sticking to our timeline. Let's become writers of our word. It's time to consider some of our habits when writing, something that Moe needs to learn. Nothing should get in the way of doing the job, especially our own idiosyncratic energy stoppers. Here are four common energy stoppers:

1. **Having no plan.** Some people write slowly because they try to draft without a plan in mind. As a result, they stare blankly at the screen without being able to generate ideas. Remember the point of all those idea generators in Chapter 2: to create a plan that will promote writing efficiency during the drafting step. What a time waster to just sit there, pulling the hair out of your head!

2. **Trying to do everything all at once.** Another energy stopper occurs when you write and rewrite every sentence, sometimes every word, one at a time until you get it just right. This is a foolish approach for at least two reasons.

For one, how do you really know if that sentence you've just slaved over for the past five minutes is perfect until you rewrite? You might decide that you don't even need that sentence at all. I can think of a time when a telecommunications employee showed me a draft of one of his messages. It included a sentence he called "a real zinger. I gave it to him where it hurts right there! And it took me a while to write that one, but it was worth it." All I had to do was ask him whether the perfectly phrased insult was truly worth it if the reader would not get his point but instead sought ways of retaliating by escalating the situation to a pointless e-mail war that might extend from the two communicators and involve their managers and teammates. The writer no longer sounded so proud of his linguistic gymnastics, admitting that he'd be better off deleting the sly comment. Thus, he wasted a lot of time on a sentence he never used.

Another reason for not editing while writing is that spending too much time on a few words or sentences jeopardizes your chances of recalling everything you need to get in the document, even with a plan. If you've ever lost your train of thought when speaking by digressing from the gist of your story to explain a minute detail, you'd know what I mean. By the time you've finished explaining the detail, you ask, "Now where was I?", losing the immediacy of the story and possibly your motivation for telling it. Since we speak three or four times faster than we write, imagine how more likely you are to run into this problem when writing.

3. **Making of the message more than it really is**. Many people over-romanticize writing. True, we want our writing to be an accurate reflection of our thinking, so we want to "get it right," whatever that means. But we're not competing for the Nobel Prize in literature. We're simply informing people about something they need to know or do. We do this in speech all the time, though it's not always easy. How, for instance, should we tell our boss that she has to do something? That's no easy task if we don't want to look like complainers, troublemakers, or wise guys. Nevertheless, we should reckon with the fact that we write the first draft only for ourselves, as Figure 2-1 in Chapter 2 indicates.

4. **Worrying**. Some people just sweat the details for their own hidden reasons. While some of their worrying results from an admitted weakness in writing skills, I have seen many writers with a good command of language struggle through drafts just as much as weaker writers. What causes this is known only by the writers themselves, if they know the reason at all. Perhaps they were traumatized by their parents' harping on the importance of writing. Maybe they were ill trained by their elementary teachers into believing that mistakes in the first draft are intolerable. Possibly they've become intimidated by the truth that they're not as good at writing as the masters they frequently read. But none of these

is an acceptable excuse. They've got to get over their parents' influence, they've got to learn another way since what their teachers taught them may not have helped, and they've got to stop comparing themselves with the masters, just like they don't compare themselves to Tiger Woods when golfing, Aretha Franklin when singing, or Barack Obama when speaking. Better yet, they've got to stop blaming anyone but themselves for nonperformance. They need to compare themselves only to themselves at their best. That's where they want to be, in maximum performance, on the verge of realizing the accomplishments they described during the treat and the trick in Chapter 1.

The value of employing the writing process is priceless. Understanding that writing occurs in steps gives us as writers the opportunity to plan, draft, revise, edit, and proofread our documents at different times. If, for example, we are involved in a project report that is due in two months, we can use today to block in our planner an hour for the planning step for 30 days from today, the drafting step over two hour-long periods 40 days from today, and the rewriting steps over a two-hour period 45 days from today. With a completely revised draft two weeks before the due date, we now can schedule a document review meeting with teammates 10 days before the due date and have plenty of time to make changes. Even if we have one final, unfinished section because the data is not complete, we still are well ahead of schedule with the bulk of the project. Writing efficiency emerges from understanding the relationship between time and the writing process. Drafting is a waste of time without a plan. Editing sentences is a waste of time without having all the information in front of you.

The two drafting techniques I'm about to describe, *free-writing* and *dialoguing*, can easily be seen as one and the same; alternatively, one can be seen as superior to the other. What should matter is the technique that works better for you or maybe invent a combination of both, as I have done on occasion. I have used them both to a considerable measure of success—if we measure success by writing a draft as quickly as possible without regard for quality. With your plan in front of you, try both to see which works for you, but be aware that your choice may change from one to the other depending on the nature of the writing assignment and the audience you're trying to reach.

Free-Writing

When discussing the writing process in Chapter 2, I described drafting as driving with SUV (*speed, uniformity,* and *volume*) while performing a constant balancing act between our interdependent creative and critical sides. Since the idea during this step is to write nonstop (speed) while staying on the topic (uniformity) to attain quantity, not quality (volume), let's look at how we can optimize drafting and then see some illustrations of how it might play out in real work situations.

Write for a set time. I hesitate to say how much time would be right for any given situation because some of us type faster than others. Also, some of us write quick requests and responses all day long, what I would call the free level of writing, requiring little prompting, planning, and rewriting. The length of time depends on how much time you actually have, your experience free-writing, and how you're feeling. Usually, 30 minutes is a long stretch of time to free-write anything, but people who don't write regularly may find a half-hour exceedingly long. The important point is to get into the habit of saying, "For the next ten minutes, I'll be writing that draft." You'll see how much time even a rough draft takes. As I mentioned in Chapter 1, people who type so many words a minute when copying will not produce the same output when writing off the top of their head.

Write nonstop with a focus on speed. This does not mean that you should frantically pursue velocity. You've got to feel relaxed. The point is not to stop, to get into a writing groove, and then the words come. You can compare this to walking a mile. If you start at a faster pace than you can maintain, you'll find that you'll have to stop from time to time. The slower but steadier pace is better and ultimately faster. Think of the story of the tortoise and the hare. There's a lot of truth in that fable!

Aim for quantity, not quality. Remember that you already have a plan that you can return to, so do not fret over issues like purposefulness, organization, grammar, or spelling. Just get all your ideas down for now. On the other hand, if you have a strong idea about the structure of your message, as many of us often do, then you should write with every tool available to you, including up-front purpose statements, paragraphing, headings, bullet points, and topic sentences. If all this sounds foreign to you, don't worry about it. We'll look at this stuff in Chapter 4.

Now think small, as you did when thinking about the treat and the trick in Chapter 1. Don't think about writing a 200-page user manual; think about something far smaller, say, a meeting announcement in which you'll state the logistics (time, date, and place), the meeting chair, the meeting purpose, invitees, four agenda items, suggestions for participation, and a closing RSVP. You suddenly remember that you need to write this message, which might look like this:

Humphrey Hudson of the Marketing Team will hold a meeting on Wednesday, September 2, 2:00 P.M.–3:00 P.M., in Conference Room 3, to discuss proposals for

> launching the Bilbao Base. Representatives from Finance, Information Systems, Legal, Merchandising, and Sales should attend. The agenda will include the Marshall Proposal, the Fuller Proposal, the Rehnquist Proposal, and the Kickoff Plan. We invite your ideas on these items. Please e-mail us the names of attendees from your group before 11:00 A.M. Friday. Thank you.

That's not a challenging message to draft. It contains only 81 words and 6 sentences, yet in that brief e-mail the writer includes all the necessary information. The organization could be better. For instance, the third sentence ("The agenda will include . . .") could have begun a new paragraph and a bullet list, and the fourth sentence ("We invite your ideas . . .") could have been in the beginning of the message, but the writer cared only about getting everything down. It will do for now. Assuming the writer had all the information at the top of her head and is a decent typist, she would have typed those 81 words in two minutes or so. Slower typists would need four to six minutes, making the same assumption about knowing their content.

Think for a minute about the readers. As simple as this message is, it has a large and important audience across the organization. This being the case, the writer will want to spend a bit more time rewriting it, primarily for structure, but the revision will be a cinch because she has everything in front of her without having lost a minute. Otherwise, how would she know what needs fixing unless she has something to fix? She might rewrite the e-mail like this:

Humphrey Hudson of the Marketing Team invites your ideas on the proposals for launching the Bilbao Base. He will hold a meeting on Wednesday, September 2, 2:00 P.M.–3:00 P.M., in Conference Room 3, and representatives from Finance, Information Systems, Legal, Merchandising, and Sales should attend.

The agenda is as follows:

- Marshall Proposal
- Fuller Proposal
- Rehnquist Proposal
- Kickoff Plan

Please e-mail us the names of attendees from your group before 11:00 A.M. Friday. Thank you.

The improvement in purposefulness and structure will be more appealing to her readers. But we're getting ahead of ourselves; we'll be taking a close look at rewriting in Chapter 4.

Continue thinking small. Assume a specific audience, trying your hand at writing for a set time, say, five minutes, as steadily as you can on any of the topics in Figure 3-3. And don't plan! Just write without correcting or second-guessing yourself. Get the sense of what five minutes really feels like. A lot can get done in five minutes; on the other hand, staring blankly at a blank screen or piece of paper can seem endless. So, again, here are the rules:

1. Start with Topic 1.

2. Don't spend any time planning these topics—as soon as you read one, start writing.

FIGURE 3-3: Free-Writing Exercises

Note: If two different readers you've chosen are actually the same person (e.g., your manager is your chief executive, your manager is your friend, or your friend is your coworker on the same level), write to that person the way you normally would.

#	Topic	Reader	Time	Words
1	a description of your past (personal, academic, professional, or any other side of you)	yourself	3 mins.	
2	a description of your present (personal, academic, professional, or any other side of you)	yourself	4 mins.	
3	a description of your future plans (personal, academic, professional, or any other side of you)	yourself	5 mins.	
4	a description of your office	a friend	5 mins.	
5	a book or movie you'd recommend	a friend	5 mins.	
6	a day trip or activity you'd recommend	a friend	5 mins.	
7	a description of a detailed procedure you perform	a coworker on your level	4 mins.	
8	a report on what you accomplished your last workday	your manager	4 mins.	
9	a course or seminar you wish to take	a coworker on your level	6 mins.	
10	an analysis of the state of your business	your manager	6 mins.	
11	an ideal location for a staff retreat	your chief executive	6 mins.	
12	a suggestion for a new employee benefit	your chief executive	6 mins.	

3. Time yourself for precisely the allotted minutes.

4. Write nonstop—remember, not rushed, but relaxed.

5. Resist the urge to correct any errors.

6. Write with the suggested reader in mind.

7. Count the words you produced after five minutes are up.

(Word-processing programs have automatic word counters you can click on to perofrm this chore.)

8. Read the next paragraphs before trying a second topic.

Ask yourself these SUV questions about your experience:

Speed

1. Was it easy or difficult to create a steady stream of words?

2. Did the flow occur immediately? If not, at what point did it occur? If yes, did it occur from the first moment? a few moments into the session? after a particular idea popped into your head?

3. How did you feel physically while writing? If you were uncomfortable, why? If you were comfortable, what exactly were you doing? Can you repeat the technique where you write at work?

4. How did you feel emotionally while writing? If you felt stressed, why? If you felt good, what did you do differently from the times that you felt stressed?

Uniformity

5. Did your content stick to the point? If not, how much of it strayed? If it did, was relying on the central point helpful to you?

6. How far down in the draft is your most important point? How long did it take you to get to the point? If you started with the most important point, did it help you stick to a cohesive narrative? If your most important point appears farther down, is the information preceding it irrelevant? Out of place?

Volume

7. How many words did you produce? (Keep a record in the right column of Figure 3-3 to chart your progress as you get more practice.)

8. How many words per minute did you produce? (Divide the word count by the number of minutes.)

Repeat the process, doing as many of the assignments as you can to compare word counts. Don't do more than three or four at any one time because fatigue will set in, nullifying any points of comparison. Ask the same SUV questions for each topic. Were some topics harder than others? If yes, this may be simply the result of your not being well informed about the topic and nothing more—not because of some writing insecurity or personal deficiency. If some topics caused a different physical or emotional response, why do you think that was the case?

If they were all relatively easy, no trouble to keep a steady flow of words, stick to the point, and feel relaxed, then I can assure you that you are well on your way to being an efficient drafter, if you're not one already.

If you feel that you've accomplished something special here, then keep bringing on topics of your own, topics that relate to the writing you do at work. Practice those over no more than five to seven minutes. As you find that you're maxing out on words per minute, move to longer periods of 10 to 15 minutes, and then longer, always keeping word counts. You will see an improvement in your word production.

Dialoguing

The second drafting practice is one that emerges from idea generator 3 in Chapter 2: Ask it. In fact, you may look at idea generator 3 and dialoguing as interdependent techniques. The main difference between the two is that the idea generator will give you just a list of ideas, whereas dialoguing will give you complete sentences, even if they are somewhat disjointed. Remember, all that matters is getting down all your thoughts. And just as with free-writing, you're thinking speed, uniformity, and volume, but with dialoguing you're speaking with and listening to your audience. Here's how it works:

Start talking with your fingers. Imagine yourself in a conversation with the intended audience of your document. As they sit before you, begin the dialogue: "We're here to talk about . . . I need your help . . . This is how it would work."

Answer their questions, again with your fingers. Respond to questions that you think each audience member would have as the document progresses: "How long has this been a problem? By what standard are you measuring the problem? What's the impact of the problem? Who would train the person assigned to the task? What are our options? How much would it cost? Are there hidden costs?" If you don't know the answer, at least write the questions, so you'll remember to address them later.

Using the earlier call for a meeting, this is how dialoguing would work:

Audience: What's up?

Writer: Humphrey Hudson of the Marketing Team invites your ideas on the proposals for launching the Bilbao Base.

Audience: How?

Writer: He will hold a meeting.

Audience: When?

Writer: Wednesday, September 2, from 2:00 P.M. to 3:00 P.M.

Audience: Where?

Writer: Conference Room 3.

Audience: Who else is invited?

Writer: Representatives from Finance, Information Systems, Legal, Merchandising, and Sales

Audience: What will we discuss?

Writer: The Marshall Proposal, the Fuller Proposal, the Rehnquist Proposal, and the Kickoff Plan.

Audience: How do we confirm our attendance?

Writer: Please e-mail us the names of attendees from your group before 11:00 A.M. Friday.

Audience: OK.

Writer: Thank you.

In reality, the writer would be writing not the audience's questions but just the writer's answers. The draft would actually look like this:

Humphrey Hudson of the Marketing Team invites your ideas on the proposals for launching the Bilbao Base.

He will hold a meeting.

Wednesday, September 2, 2:00 P.M.–3:00 P.M.

Conference Room 3.

Representatives from Finance, Information Systems, Legal, Merchandising, and Sales.

The Marshall Proposal, the Fuller Proposal, the Rehnquist Proposal, and the Kickoff Plan.

Please e-mail us the names of attendees from your group before 11:00 A.M. Friday.

Thank you.

All the writer has to do now is add connecting words and phrases. The added words below are italicized.

Humphrey Hudson of the Marketing Team invites your ideas on the proposals for launching the Bilbao Base. He will hold a meeting *on* Wednesday, September 2, 2:00 P.M.–3:00 P.M., *in* Conference Room 3, *and* representatives from Finance, Information Systems, Legal, Merchandising, and Sales *should attend.*

The agenda is as follows:

- Marshall Proposal
- Fuller Proposal
- Rehnquist Proposal
- Kickoff Plan

Please e-mail us the names of attendees from your group before 11:00 A.M. Friday. Thank you.

I like using this technique, partly because I often hear documents in dialogue form, even the most technical of documents, and partly because it helps eliminate a step later in the writing process, namely looking for missed details. If I take the time to imagine what questions my audience will ask, I will have an easier time in the rewriting step.

Now you have a sense of direction that comes out of a plan based on any number of idea generators described in Chapter 2. In using any of these IGs, you are acknowledging that the brain is far quicker than the fingers, so you need a trick or two to capture all your ideas, break through writer's block, and get those fingers moving. You are also armed with the means of acceleration coming from the drafting techniques described in this chapter, designed to give your first drafts speed, uniformity, and volume. You also have a resolute mindset that comes from asking the Three Big Questions: Where am I going? When must I get there? How will I get there? You can answer these questions when planning: I'm writing a justification for purchasing XYZ, I'll start by listing it, and I'll plan for 3 minutes. And you can answer these questions when drafting: I will complete a finished draft for revision, I'll draft for 15 minutes, and I'll free-write the draft. That's looking at writing like a writer. You've got the tools and the toughness. Now you're getting there.

4

Strength—Standing Fast in the Midst of Chaos

(Moe enters Didi's office as she is writing a report.)

Moe: I just e-mailed you the draft of the conference report.

Didi: It's 10:15. You said you'd get it to me by 10:30. You beat the clock.

Moe: Wait. You haven't read it yet.

(Didi opens his e-mail, downloads the three-page file, scans it in five seconds, and returns to her report.)

Didi: It's fine.

Moe: How would you know?

Didi: After all we've talked about, there's no way you'd get it to me for review before the deadline unless you felt it was a workable draft.

Moe: I'm not so sure about that.

Didi: I am.

It often happens like this. Many people are quick to say that their improvement goes unnoticed by their managers, but my experience as a writing consultant who has spoken to hundreds of managers tells me otherwise: Managers notice the improvement in their staff before the staff does. The dialogue above shows this to be the case with Mopey Moe. Speedy Didi is thrilled that he has gotten the rough draft to her on time. Sure, it may not be perfect, but just by scrolling at lightning speed through his draft, she is sure that he has captured relevant content from all six sessions of the conference and that he structured that content logically. Most important for Didi, Moe has taken care of the most time-consuming part of the writing process: the planning and the drafting. He has dealt with the hard part. All Didi has to do is fix whatever Moe has given her. Finally, Moe has shown Didi something he hadn't shown her until that moment—an "I'll get this done" attitude, an attitude that feeds on itself, implanting in him a seed of confidence that will flower, grow taller, and shine brighter with every new document he writes.

All managers who understand writing know that creating a message from scratch is when most of the work gets done; that's why they have their subordinates do it. If managers drafted every message for their department, they'd be writing 24-7 with no time for managing other responsibilities. So their staff perform the time-consuming task of planning and drafting, and the managers revise the drafts to suit the departmental message and their personal or organizational style. Then once subordinates turn out workable drafts, their managers begin counting on them for more, and the more they write, the better they become. For this reason,

I often tell employees not to be upset when their manager red-marks their drafts. As long as their manager keeps asking them for more, they are still the go-to person for that manager. That's what counts—they have a value to their team.

This book opened with a seemingly impossible scenario. You're physically down, you've got tons of things to write in no time, the environment around you is in chaos, and the people around you are making it worse. It's one thing to have the resolve (the treats and the tricks), the tools (the writing process, the seven IGs, the two drafting techniques), and the toughness (the Three Big Questions) to get the job done, and we know that's all well and good in theory. But, in practice, how do you pull it all off when your body is caving in and the world around you is crashing? It takes herculean strength to stand fast and do what has to be done in the midst of chaos.

The strength I'm talking about is strength you can develop. If Chapters 2 and 3 are about the tools you need to write fast, then Chapters 4 and 5 are about how to use those tools, how to become fit and stay fit, so to speak, so you can maximize those tools. This chapter looks at strength-building from two angles: reaching yourself by cultivating your own attitudes and habits related to writing, and reaching them, your readers, by delivering quality documents under tight time pressures.

Building a Writer's World

Strength as a writer means having a strong attitude in approaching writing and a good system when delivering the final product. Writing is as physical an activity as it is a mental one. Writing a lot might not give you the physique of a bodybuilder, but take a moment to think about how capable a writer you are with a 103-degree body temperature, or on heavy doses of ibuprofen to make that back pain go away, or when exhausted from cleaning that messy office, or attending back-to-back-to-back meetings all day. I'm not trying to make excuses for poor performance or missed deadlines—I'm simply stating a fact about myself and most other people I know. We need physical strength (stamina) and mental strength (fortitude) to write lengthy documents like formal proposals, audit reports, and evaluative reports under pressure. Sure, basic writing skills are important, but many writers with good technical abilities fall short of meeting deadlines or handling multiple writing projects.

Time and again, I meet businesspeople from all fields whose excellent writing skills do little to prevent them from caving in under tight time constraints. They write fluently enough to satisfy most managers, but they feel undue stress when writing or they struggle needlessly through first drafts. In fact, their pursuit of perfection often inhibits their ability to write quickly. They may prefer writing one perfect sentence after another to delivering a purposeful, complete message, thereby delaying essential communication. Or they may start with a Mopey Moe attitude: "I can't get this done with the best quality, so I'll just have to plan it forward or not do it at all." They need to change their lives, to rethink the importance they place on writing—which is to say not that writing is unimportant but that their making it important should put them to work, not psychologically paralyze them.

Intense focus and consistent endurance generate success—physical actions, not mere thoughts. Thus, the key is to develop a system for maximizing creativity and improving efficiency. Changing the world in which you write starts with changing yourself, changing your surroundings, state of mind, physical condition, and social network. We'll look at these domains—our environmental, mental, physical, and social states—one at a time.

Environmental Issues

Writing fast requires an ability to get started comfortably any-where—trains, buses, libraries, waiting rooms, wherever. You might not be able to alter the environment where you find yourself writing, and in some cases you might have more power than you think. A look at some situations writers face at work can be helpful in determining which have a positive and which a negative impact on your performance.

Check lighting, temperature, ventilation, and noise levels. To promote writing efficiency, use whatever influence you have to control your surroundings. Your writing environment is directly linked to your productivity. Three overarching issues arise here. The first is the inclination to say that checking environmental controls is too obvious to merit attention. The second is the claim that the environment does not have any substantive effect on writing productivity. And the third is that we have minimal control over these issues when writing in a leased or borrowed space. The answer to these three claims can be countered in one simple Speedy Didi-ism: If you think it affects writing productivity, then it does—so control what you can as best you can.

Lighting might not always be in your control, but proper lighting is essential not only for your vision but for your psyche. If you haven't heard about seasonal affective disorder (SAD), the mood disorder resulting from light deprivation, typically in winter, then you ought to notice how the temperament of most people—including you—changes to a duller shade of brightness or a deeper hue of somber, depending on whether you're an optimist or a pessimist, as the daylight hours dwindle with the falling leaves. While artificial light is no substitute for natural light, it's better than no light at all. In fact, where I do most of my writing, I must draw the blinds in the early morning because my windows face east, so the early sun pours in and floods my computer screen. As much as I enjoy the sun washing me with its morning warmth, I sadly turn on the lights, shut the blinds, and start writing until the sun rises over the window, when I pull up the blinds. Unless drawing the blinds is necessary to keep the glare away from the screen or you suffer from a skin problem whose antidote is shelter from direct sunlight, let the sunshine in. As for the light of your computer, keep a reasonable distance from the monitor to prevent eye irritation. However, if you notice that you're straining, squinting, or hunching forward to read the screen or keyboard, back up. You can always enlarge the view, which, for practical purposes, is preferable to enlarging the font size. Robert, an IT professional from a power company, taught me about the flickering rate of most monitors, something that is imperceptible to many people. As Microsoft says, "a flickering monitor can contribute to eyestrain and headaches." Robert recommends adjusting the screen resolution and refresh rates to manage the screen flickering issue. The help function of your computer operating system should specify those ideal resolutions and rates, which vary by monitor.

The ideal temperature is clearly a matter of preference, but heating things up in the winter and cooling them down in the summer contribute toward keeping a writer on task. I have seen writers in large office areas use space heaters and miniature fans to get comfortable while writing. Shelia, who works for a commercial bank as a sales manager in a branch office in New Jersey, sits close to the bank entrance, which by her estimate swings open and closed at least 300 to 400 times a day. That amounts to a lot of Arctic blasts in the winter and tropical humid gusts in the summer. Shelia's solution: powering a three-pound, dual-speed, oscillating electric space heater by her legs, usually the first part of the body to go numb when sitting for long periods, as she does. These heaters have thermostats to prevent overheating and to save on the electric bill. At $50 to $100, they are worth the price to maintain a steady writing pace. Portable air conditioners, on the other hand, are considerably more expensive, prohibitive at Shelia's salary since her company does not pick up the cost of these extras. She explains that an old-fashioned but quiet tower fan positioned on a credenza some six feet from the side of her chair does the job of consistently and unobtrusively circulating the air conditioning in the summer as the entrance door keeps opening and closing. These fans run as low as $25 and generally no more than $50, while a portable air conditioner could cost ten times as much.

Proper ventilation is another area of concern. Using a fan to move the air around increases the comfort level, but it might not be enough to control for risks resulting from exposure to fumes, smoke, and unpleasant odors. The American Lung Association suggests that exhaust fans address this issue. Among its recommendations are to keep the ventilation apparatus free of obstructions and to position yourself away from the line of air moving toward the exhaust system. In addition, heating and air conditioning representatives admonish their clients to keep their area as airtight as possible. This means checking for drafts and making sure those things that should close, such as doors and windows, do close.

Productive writers have learned as many ways to deal with noise as noisemakers have learned to make noise, yet the best way to deal with noise is purely a matter of preference. Ernest Hemingway was a big fan of writing early in the morning because of the silence it brought to the writing process. Some 40 years later, another Nobel Prize laureate, Toni Morrison, said she also gets up early to write in isolation and silence. On the other hand, novelist and professor Edmund White has written, "I've never willingly written a word without listening to music of some sort." Twentieth-century Swiss theologian Karl Barth thrilled to the sound of

Mozart as he composed his magnum opus, the 13-volume, 8,300-page, 6 million-word *Church Dogmatics*.

Turning to successful workplace writers, my informal surveys of hundreds of people indicate that most are easily distracted, preferring silence to music. Some who work in relatively hectic environments say that using their portable music devices, such as iPods, iPhones, or MP3 players, helps them tune out unwanted noise and tune in pleasant music. Listening to music through headphones can cause other distractions, compromising output. I recently met three investment analysts who were writing equity research reports while listening to music through their headphones. Their manager told me he was pleased with their production, so they must be doing something right. Meanwhile, a young man from a different brokerage firm who is about the same age as the three musically minded writers and who is enamored of electronic gadgets steers clear of them when writing and pops in ear plugs to block out sound distractions. The music, he says, would get in the way of his composing. His boss said that she appreciated his output of the same types of documents. The important thing is to think about these issues and see what works best for you—silence, song, or something in between.

Make ergonomic improvements. Do you suffer from neck, shoulder, or back pain after long periods of writing at your desk? Since the human body is not designed to endure sedentary positions for hours on end, and since many of us do not have a choice but to perform this arduous task, knowledge of ergonomic principles can prove indispensable in improving and maintaining writing speed.

A quick stop at the International Ergonomics Association (IEA) website would be a good start. IEA divides ergonomics into three general categories or domains: physical (e.g., posture, repetitive movements, workplace layout), cognitive (e.g., human-computer interaction, workload, technical skills), and organizational (e.g., workplace design, working times, project design). In a sense, this book requires that you have a working knowledge of ergonomics because writers need to be as comfortable as possible when sketching ideas or tapping away at the keyboard.

On the physical side of ergonomics, you might answer these questions: Is your chair comfortably suited to your body? Is it adjustable to whatever position you choose to sit? Is it sufficiently elevated relative to the keyboard? Is the keyboard itself easy to the touch? Is it easy to maneuver through various functions? When your fingers are aching, do you take a needed rest? If you answer no to any of these questions, what modifications can you make to change things? Getting in the right state of body should precede even getting in the right state of mind so that you do not sluggishly and mindlessly plow ahead, eroding valuable production time.

As for the cognitive side, is there anything you can do to make yourself more technologically proficient? Are there any shortcuts you can learn to make that instant text pop up when you need it? Is there an intuitive program that decreases the number of steps you need to take as you maneuver through monotonous and mechanical steps on the computer? These and other issues directly relate to the physical demands of writing, so learning the technical skills and using the best programs and hardware come into play here.

Finally, how do organizational ergonomics affect writing speed? According to the IEA, the impact is huge. The layout of a project plan can by itself doom any attempt at writing efficiency. Do the project partners have immediate, easy access to each other? Are the tasks designed to eliminate redundancy where it is useless and to incorporate it where it is useful? Would telecommuting increase writing output? Does the design of the office space promote writing fluency? The space before and even beyond the writer should be as attractive as possible to get the fingers moving forward. After all, writing is not just a part of the work that most office workers do; it *is* the work. Therefore, if you can do something to improve your safety, comfort, ease of use, productivity, and aesthetics—the five pillars of ergonomics—then do it!

Reduce clutter. Loose papers accumulate quickly on desks, shelves, drawers, file cabinets, and window sills, and for many people they become as difficult to remove as squatters in tenements once they get comfortable in the strength of their growing numbers. They create a life of their own, each piece of paper coming with its unique story about why you need to keep it exactly where it is. And you do, because it's easier to leave them alone than to argue with them. You can't find a new home for them, so you leave them right in front of your face all day long, convincing yourself that you can live harmoniously with that unreturned letter from Aunt Mary, that to-do list you need to refigure, that new insurance application that you'll get to sooner or later, those two books you'll start reading any day now—and where is that software CD you thought you left on the top of the pile? You're sure you left it there. Maybe a coworker took it. Someone always seems to be messing with your pile because you know exactly where you left everything. You know darn well there's a method to your madness if only people wouldn't mess with your stuff. If you could only find that CD now! But why did you need it in the first place?

If you've ever been in a place like this one, try clearing your field of vision by removing those papers from your desk—now. You've just improved your mental health. Now you will surely find that after removing all those stacks, something remains on the desk: a thick layer of dust. Go ahead, blow it away. Now you've just improved your physical health, to boot.

On the other hand, say you know with all your heart and mind that there really are valuable things in that six-foot-high stack on your desk—if only you could find them—then you have another alternative, one that a consultant friend of mine, Barrett J. Mandel, used to suggest in his time-management classes: Turn the stack upside down. Now the stuff on the top of the stack is ancient. It's much easier to go through the stack now. The first sheet is about a conference you've long ago decided not to attend, the second sheet is about an expired program, the third about an expired person, and so on. Plenty of stuff you can chuck right away. Then you get into a search-and-destroy mood and cut through a whole heap of annoying paper.

Surround yourself with beauty. The idea is to bring into the environment *anything* that might stimulate thinking: aphorisms, artwork, nature photography—anything. I have gone through numerous stages myself: prints of Ansel Adams's black-and-white photographs of America's majestic West, Piet Mondrian's minimalist line paintings, Richard Diebenkorn's bright abstract Ocean Park landscape series, the jazz photographs of William P. Gottlieb or Herman Leonard. Then there was a time when I covered my walls with famous quotations, among my favorite being George Santayana's "By nature's kindly disposition most questions which it is beyond a man's power to answer do not occur to him at all"; Albert Camus's "Integrity needs no rules"; Benjamin Franklin's "One today is worth two tomorrows"; Albert Einstein's "I never think of the future. It comes soon enough"; Duke Ellington's "I don't need time. What I need is a deadline"; Nicholas Murray Butler's "Many people's tombstones should read, 'Died at 30. Buried at 60'"; Eric Hoffer's "People who bite the hand that feeds them usually lick the boot that kicks them"; Teresa of Avila's "More tears are shed over answered prayers than unanswered ones";

James Thurber's "It is better to know some of the questions than all of the answers"; Isaac Bashevis Singer's "Every creator painfully experiences the chasm between his inner vision and its ultimate expression"; and Friedrich Nietzsche's "The surest way to corrupt a young man is to teach him to esteem more highly those who think alike than those who think differently." But now I prefer just images or artistic gifts of family and friends, whether it be an aboriginal calendar from an Australian cousin, trinkets like the hand-painted wooden spoon a former coworker brought for me from her trip to Russia, a shot glass from a hokey tourist trap in Miami given to me by a student, a brightly painted hummingbird on tree bark a friend bought for me from a street vendor in Aca-pulco, 5×4-inch oil paintings created by my daughters during their elementary school years—all gifts I treasure as endowments of love from special people.

Think about things you really like, perhaps a work by an artist like Chuck Close, whose prolific output continues in spite of an arterial spinal collapse 20 years ago that has virtually paralyzed him from the neck down. How can Mopey Moe dare complain about his own problems after reflecting on Close's artistic achievements in spite of the odds against him? Or get nature photography, espe-cially of industrious ants, which carry 10 times their body weight, or worker bees, which won't stop in their mission of collecting pollen at the service of the queen's brood. Those images should keep you moving. Or, just like a worker bee yourself, collect favor-ite aphorisms of your own, whether they be Yogisms, religious proverbs, or inspirational quotes from the world of government, military, sports, culinary arts, or literature—it doesn't matter what, as long as they work for you. You are the creator of your environment; take ownership of it.

As a cautionary note, some employers may frown upon expres-sions of individuality in the workplace, including displaying any personal items in the work area. Some supervisors could form negative opinions of such employees, inferring they do not take their jobs seriously, whereas other employers don't seem to mind, provided they produce quality work. If you're not sure whether your employer will mind, observe your colleagues' work spaces and make your best attempt to follow suit while maintaining your own sense of individuality without offending anyone.

Mental Issues

Even the fastest writers among us can be slowed down when they've forgotten the meaning of a particular word they need to use or if they can't find an appropriate synonym or antonym for a word. Depending on the nature of the document, there may be peculiar grammatical and stylistic rules that you may be unfamiliar with or can't remember correctly. Following many of these tips should help quicken your pace when you've hit a tough patch.

Keep good reference books nearby. What books does Speedy Didi keep within an arm's reach of her writing command-and-control center? The usual writer's references like a dictionary, thesaurus, and grammar and style book, for sure. Each has its unique benefits: You can't get definitions of words in a grammar and style book or thesaurus, synonyms in a dictionary or grammar and style book, or grammar tips in a dictionary or thesaurus. All three are necessary, as are their electronic counterparts. (More about online resources in a moment.) Those pocket-sized, abridged versions won't do, either. Didi is a pro. She sees them as seriously limited and incapable of replacing the real thing, the way butchers wouldn't trade in their heavy-duty knives for common kitchen varieties, and doctors would never replace their medical references with popular medical trade books.

Which ones would work best for you? Plenty are available from your favorite bookstore or shopping website. Should you get Houghton-Mifflin's *American Heritage Dictionary* or the *Oxford English Dictionary?* Is *Roget's International Thesaurus* any better than *Webster's New World Thesaurus*, or would the *Rodale Synonym Finder* do? Which grammar and style book is best: *Gregg Reference Manual, Harbrace College Handbook, Little, Brown Handbook, Random House Handbook, St. Martin's Handbook*, or any from the host of others that virtually every reputable publisher reprints every few years? That's up to you—they're all good. Just have these essential resources close by and make sure they don't become dust collectors.

There are other must-have books for serious writers, as well. A book of quotations is indispensable when you're called upon to deliver speeches or write articles or just looking for inspiration on a writing topic. *Bartlett's Familiar Quotations* and *The Viking Book of Aphorisms* are just two of many excellent references that draw from literature, politics, and popular culture. *The Forbes Book of Business Quotations* is an excellent source not only from businesspeople but from entertainers, writers, philosophers, and creative minds from numerous disciplines, divided by topic and indexed by author of the quotation.

If presenting or publishing formal papers for work, professional development, or school is a priority, then you'll need a citation stylebook like the *MLA Handbook* (Modern Language Association of America), *Publication Manual of the American Psychological Association* (APA Stylebook), *Chicago Manual of Style*, or its sister publication, *A Manual for Writers of Research Papers, Theses, and Dissertations*. Which one you choose depends on the reader's requirements. For instance, my dissertation committee called for the *Chicago Manual of Style*, but I have published articles requiring MLA style and others requiring APA style. Each business, journal, university, and professor has a formatting standard, so be sure to check before making the investment. In fact, many fields have their own stylebooks. For instance, the U.S. Air Force relies on *The Tongue and the Quill*, the legal profession refers to *The Blue Book*, engineers prefer the *IEEE Standards Style Manual*, and many journalists go to *The AP Stylebook* (Associated Press), *New York Times Manual of Style and Usage,* or *The Wall Street Journal Stylebook* to resolve issues ranging from pronoun and adjective-adverb confusion to punctuation, number usage, capitalization, and abbreviation. Knowing that so many excellent references are available, you should have at least one stylebook for when the need arises.

Bookmark electronic resources. No one likes books more than I do, but Speedy Didi would be the first person to remind me—and certainly the one to educate Mopey Moe—about the lightning speed at which we can reference online writers' resources. The truth is, you probably can look up *adz, auslaut, ambivert, apocope,* and *aleatory* online faster than you can flip through the pages of your beloved dictionary—so when speed matters, go to www.dictionary.com. The publishers of some of the books I just mentioned have online databases available for comprehensive and customized searches, and some reference books are available in their entirety as PDF files. If you prefer, you can also download language software packages that can also do the job of most print references.

In this Wikipedia world, all it takes to resolve disputes about *that* or *which, who* or *whom, I* or *myself, affect* or *effect,* and the comma or semicolon is a quick check in your favorite search engine—Google, Yahoo Search, whatever. Type in the term you're searching to discover how many authorities have checked in on that topic. Most of the entries are quite reliable, coming from university writing centers or reputable publishers and authors.

Pocket-sized electronic language tools, such as dictionaries, thesauruses, translators, and grammar books, are also pervasive. Better yet, download these applications on your BlackBerry or iPhone for those free moments in restaurants and cafés, taxis, buses, or waiting rooms so that you can always have access to these invaluable guides.

Believe in yourself. Lacking confidence in your ability to get the job done successfully will slow down your writing, causing you to miss important deadlines. Having confidence goes well beyond the groundless "I believe in myself" comment that the least confident or competent communicators untruthfully say about themselves. Making this statement demands that you can back it up: *"I believe in myself* because I've made a hundred deadlines before . . . *I believe in myself* because I could not have gotten this far in the company without being a winner . . . *I believe in myself* because if I can say the darn thing, then I can write it."

Speedy Didi is one for creative visualization, picturing herself actually in the process of writing productively, of completing what she has set out to write before she even writes it and anticipating the great feeling she'll have when she types that last key and proclaims "Done!" This mindset is in no way akin to daydreaming. Let's call daydreaming making believe you're someone you're not, or doing something you can't, or being somewhere you're not. Creative visualization, on the other hand, is imagining yourself in possession of something you can possess, engaging in an activity you're capable of, and achieving something you can. You're not trying to be anyone other than yourself when you are at your productive very best. Didi has read and bought into all those books on positive thinking by Napoleon Hill, Dale Carnegie, Norman Vincent Peale, Wayne Dyer, Deepak Chopra, Eckhart Tolle, and many others. In fact, she's the sort of person who is willing to try anything that will help her improve—and if you are that sort of person, you too will improve.

Count the number of words you produce. Think for a moment about people you've noticed writing at a breakneck pace. They seem to glide effortlessly from one page to the next, producing sentences, paragraphs, and messages that get the job done. That's what Mopey Moe sees when he passes Speedy Didi's desk as she blazes through one procedure after a proposal after a report while he's still dwelling on his first e-mail of the day. The truth is that Moe is buying into the fallacy that Didi is a word-processing machine, something none of us really are. Instead of trusting his unreliable eyes, he should defer to his math skills by counting the words to determine how much Didi really is producing.

Word counting is not unusual among even famously successful writers. For instance, journalist and critic George Plimpton noted that Ernest Hemingway counted the words he'd written each day as a way of keeping an eye on his progress. In a radio interview, prolific political commentator William F. Buckley said that he aimed for a mere 300 words per day. By Buckley's reasoning, 300 words a day equate to a 5,000-word short story in two weeks, a novella in two months, and a novel in six months. How many writers actually create anything at the astonishing pace of 25 stories, 6 novellas, or 2 novels a year? Few if any, to be sure, but this is precisely Buckley's point. Producing 300 words is a modest goal. It amounts to a little bit more than this paragraph and the previous one. It's no more than a page-long letter or memo for a workplace writer. Starting there brings a humble sense of accomplishment and will lead to larger numbers and more documents.

Use the writing process. Since writing is done in steps—planning, drafting, rewriting—you can use the process to your benefit. You can methodically complete one step at a time in one sitting or several sittings, depending on the complexity of the writing situation. You can also eliminate unnecessary steps based on whether the writing task is free, formulaic, or fresh, as we saw in Chapter 3. Taking command of the writing process will help you feel less overwhelmed by writing projects because you will complete them one word, sentence, and paragraph at a time. It will also help you to pace yourself through complex writing tasks. In short, using the writing process wisely will increase your speed and even make you a better writer.

I remain convinced that writing skills are not something we're born with but a talent we can cultivate over time. I admit, however, that some people are better at it than others, but this fact changes nothing. No matter how early and how long we tried, few of us would have been a Kenenisa Bekele at distance running, a Michael Phelps at swimming, a Tiger Woods at golf, or a Roger Federer at tennis, but that reality does not stop many of us from participating recreationally in running, golf, or tennis or, for that matter, even performing competitively in local amateur tournaments. We just want to participate to the extent that it remains a worthwhile activity. In the same vein, we want to write at work not to become world-renowned report writers and e-mailers but to get the job done. The writing process exists for this very reason, to help us use our time quickly and write our ideas easily, by separating the creative and critical tasks of composing.

A final note about the writing process: Pace yourself. If writing is not feeling good, then take a moment to figure out why. Is it because you're trying to accomplish in one sitting more than you can? Or is it because of unclear objectives? Insufficient information about your audience? Incomplete data? Or perhaps it's the result of undue self-imposed pressure? Try focusing those questions inward, taking as much responsibility for the answer as you can without pointing fingers to the slowpokes who haven't gotten to you the information you need, the micromanaging supervisor, or the demanding client whose hurry-up-and-wait attitude you will learn to master as time passes. To get to the finish line faster, you've got to feel confident and move those fingers in synch with your thoughts. As American composer, bandleader, and pianist extraordinaire Duke Ellington said, "It don't mean a thing if it ain't got that swing."

Physical Issues

Writing is a physical activity. You will find that you can produce more words when you're at your peak performance level, meaning you're healthy, wide awake, and well fed. The tips in this section help bring your body and mind in harmony to aid you in producing more in less time.

Keep a log. Productive writers take notes of meetings attended, ideas overheard, and gems that miraculously pop into their head—wherever they are, at whatever time, however they can. They also enter data about planned, in-progress, and completed writing projects. If this sounds to you like writing for the sake of writing, not so fast. That's what writers do. They write. This note-taking practice serves a purpose far more important to the fast writer than just recording information for historical or reference reasons, as if those reasons were not enough. Actually, keeping a log is as much a physical-refining exercise as it is a mental one. Productive writers keep a log for three reasons. The obvious one is to be sure that they don't lose essential information or depend solely on their memory. Another motive is to possess that assuredness of always having something to write about. They'll never run out of things to write about if they just record the events unfolding before them. Finally, and perhaps most important, they keep a log to keep their "writer's body" in shape. This last reason is no different from why, aside from competing, Kenenisa Bekele runs a hundred miles a week, Michael Phelps swims endless laps, Tiger Woods drives from the tee and putts for hours, and Roger Federer slams dozens of serves under the watchful eye of his coach. They need to maintain that competitive edge, to be at the top of their game. Similarly, the more we write, the better we can write on demand. Just as baseball players swing in the on-deck circle before batting, as pianists run chords before performing, so do writers write just for the exercise, to sharpen their writer's instinct.

I remember having a conversation with a young ballet dancer who was on a one-month vacation in a resort area. She told me how she was not looking forward to her first week back at the ballet company because of the pain her body would have to endure as it became acclimated to the physical demands of the profession. Returning to writing after a long hiatus feels like this. It's not a stretch to say that writing is a physical task as well as a mental one. Most of us can't deal with producing words on paper or on the screen when we are exhausted or ill, but, with constant practice, spurred by keeping a log, we keep in a writing groove, in a writer's zone, and get on task right away. How important that is to writing fast!

Consider time of day. Many literary writers seem to prefer writing early in the morning, as I do. I distinctly remember, however, that once I could crank out words late into the night and until daybreak. Rare are those days now. I raise this point because, while evidence exists that morning is most conducive to writing productivity, the truth is that productivity is more linked to moments of peak energy than to time of day. This means that the graveyard-shift worker who sleeps during the late afternoon might find the evening the ideal time to breeze through drafts, while the traditional 9-to-5 employee may prefer the early morning to hammer out those lengthier messages.

Experimenting with different times of day might uncover some roadblocks you've been dealing with for a long time. Assume your normal work hours are 8:00 A.M. to 4:00 P.M. and you tend to get serious about writing those reports and proposals at the end of your shift, say, 2:00 P.M. By this time, you may have already attended a half-hour weekly staff meeting, contributed to an hourlong strategic planning teleconference session on a new project, initiated or responded to 30 routine e-mails over a two-hour period (allowing only 4 minutes per message, including reading time), spent a good hour or so researching production issues, guzzled up valuable minutes spilling into an hour when troubleshooting a frustrating technical issue with your computer and dealing with an inaccurate invoice, killed another quarter-hour reviewing a dozen purchase orders, kissed 20 minutes goodbye when coaching a teammate about the impact of tailoring a communication in either of two approaches and editing a third way, and lost more than an hour lunching with your boss and your boss's boss to review the effectiveness of how you resolved a critical issue last week. How much creativity and strength do you expect to have at 2:00 P.M.? Not a problem, you say. You'll just put in a couple extra hours to write. Big deal. You'll leave at 6:00 P.M. today. Knowing how diligent you are, you will get it done—but you would have been done a lot sooner if you were at your peak. If you had gotten into work only one hour earlier, you might not have needed to spend two extra hours writing at the end of the day when you were tired and unfocused. Finding the time of day that's right for you—your period of maximum imagination and energy—will add to your writing efficiency.

Determine duration. Another physical challenge that merits some serious reflection is the length of time one can sustain a fluent, relaxed pace. Dedicating an entire workday to nonstop writing is more than likely overdoing it because a lot of wasted time may be hidden in the cracks of those creative bursts. We saw earlier that secretaries who can type 70 words a minute know that they are not moving at this pace over an extended period of time, and they're just copying. How much more difficult is it to maintain a writing rhythm for a protracted period when you're working off the top of your head? No comparison.

So how much time drafting is too much time? Some people say 20 to 30 minutes nonstop is enough and anything more than that is just the writer fooling himself. For me, the time is more than that, up to an hour and more—even in an office environment—provided the time is undisturbed. I take some inspiration from the writing legends like novelist James Michener, who wrote some 40 books, many of them running more than a thousand pages, and who had to write for extended periods. Isaac Asimov, author of some 500 books on astoundingly varied topics, was legendary for keeping his creative juices flowing from dawn until dusk, day in and day out. Novelists like Lauran Paine and Mary Faulkner, whose volume output nearly doubled Asimov's, surely wrote all day long to produce between 750 and 900 books each. So what's the problem with writing for long stretches?

The answer to that question is obvious. People working in offices, labs, and other environments congested with people, papers, ringing phones, and pounding printers face distractions that their job demands they not ignore. All of these interruptions erode writing time. For this very reason, deciding on when to establish protected writing time and then using it effectively, even if in 15- to 30-minute loops, can help instill a writer's discipline.

Improve typing speed. Here's an obvious tip. You don't need to be a speed demon like Barbara Blackburn, who has typed as many as 212 words a minute according to the *Guinness Book of World Records*. Even Speedy Didi doesn't go that fast! Nevertheless, touch typing, not looking at the keyboard and using all your fingers, is much faster than the hunt-and peck method, by which you use two fingers and look up at the screen intermittently. In fact, a slow touch typist is usually quicker than a fairly fast hunt-and-pecker. The touch-typing method also minimizes undetected errors.

Investing in tools to improve typing speed would be a practical start. Take a typing course at a local adult school. Purchase a typing book or typing software. *Mavis Beacon Teaches Typing*, for instance, logs your progress and offers numerous activities designed to increase speed and accuracy. Earlier we looked at automatic speech recognition software, which transposes the spoken word into typed text. One of the most popular programs is *Dragon Naturally Speaking*, whose quality and accuracy have been greatly improved from previous models. While claims abound that this program can go faster than 150 words per minute, I strongly doubt whether the average person can speak that quickly and get the necessary accuracy. The bottom line is to try anything. If one technique doesn't get you going at a faster pace, then move on to something else. Just thinking about ways to improve your typing speed will move you along the path toward writing faster.

Practice planning and drafting. Just as typing practice is helpful in improving writing speed, so too is practice in planning and drafting. As noted in Chapter 2, efficient writing requires a constant mental juggling act, involving our creative and critical selves. Too much criticism early in the process reduces writing speed and compromises creativity. Therefore, it might be worthwhile to actually practice writing even when nothing is due. Whether you try one or more of the seven idea generators described in Chapter 2— canning, setting, asking, scooping, charting, posting, listing—or any other invention of your own, training through brainstorming and organizing techniques is an excellent way to spark creativity. As a reminder, you will not be writing sentences during the planning step of the writing process—just write phrases, words, or even pictures to capture your ideas and promote retention. As for drafting, try writing sentences directly on the screen, no matter how garbled they may be, over set time periods (say, five minutes) by freewriting or dialoguing (noted in Chapter 3). Check the word-count feature (all computer writing programs have it) to see how quickly you're moving with some semblance of accuracy. Compare how you've done to your previous attempts. Chances are you'll find improvements in your word-per-minute output. Consider these activities vital drills, no different from how a boxer views using the speed bag or a baseball player the batting cage to improve reflexes.

Eat well, sleep well, and exercise well. This advice mirrors what your doctor tells you during those annual checkups. All of the things that matter about taking care of yourself to prolong your life expectancy apply to writing efficiently. Overeating causes heartburn, nausea, and exhaustion, while undereating provokes hunger and distracted thinking; oversleeping brings on an undisciplined laziness, just as undersleeping induces greater susceptibility to illness, memory loss, and delirium; overexercising keeps you away from the writing desk, while underexercising puts you at risk of countless physical illnesses. As the Roman playwright Terence said, "Moderation in all things." On the surface, this advice may seem inadequate for people who have to write quickly at work, much quicker than their predecessors. But remember that writing, as well as this book, is as much about attitude as it is about technical skills. Technical skills are ineffectual in the wrong hands; however, the right hands, no matter how inexperienced or infirm they are, will get the most out of the technical skills.

Create a writing ritual. This tip can mean many different things to many different people. If, for instance, you get into work a half-hour early and crank out a draft much quicker than usual, especially after that double espresso or latte, keep getting into work early armed with that bold java. Make that method a routine in your life. Get the writing into your bloodstream as much as coffee gets in there. It doesn't have to be a time-of-day issue. Maybe it's just the way you put on headphones before you start writing, the particular music you listen to just as you start writing, a prayer you say before you start writing, or a photograph of a respected friend or family member you stare at just before you begin tapping the keys. If it works, use it. Routine is important, just as is setting the alarm, waiting for that first moment's light in the morning, or whatever it is that wakes you up. Remember, being strong as a writer demands that you have a strong command of yourself—to reach yourself at will.

Social Issues

If you are what you eat, then you are also the company you keep. Making writing a part of your social life contributes to making writing a second-nature activity. Writing communities for people of all skill levels exist in geographic locations, like your local library or community center, as well as in virtual locations, like online bulletin boards. Here are some ideas for making a writing community of your own.

Hang around writers. I am not suggesting here that you stalk John Grisham, Amy Tan, or whoever may be your favorite writer, as the Annie Wilkes character does in Stephen King's creepy tale *Misery.* All you have to do is befriend productive writers at work. Find the Speedy Didis at your job. Flatter them by saying how impressed you are with their writing ability. Ask them how they produce writing assignments so quickly and eloquently. A lot of them may say, "I don't know; it just comes natural." Irving A.

Greenfield, a writing instructor who claims to have authored some 400 books, once told me, "There are no shortcuts—just do it." When I asked author Richard Worth what he would suggest to those who want to learn to write fast, he responded, "The only way to write is to get started writing." Those suggestions may not seem helpful, but they would matter greatly to you if they came from writers whose success you witness every day on the job, as I do.

If you hang out with writers, you begin to see situations from their vantage points, you pick up ideas from them, and you begin to imitate their writing dispositions. Keep in mind I'm referring to writers at work—those most involved in daily writing assignments, those whose job it is to meet deadlines every day. While you don't have to hang out with famous writers, you can read what they have to say about writing. Countless books on the subject "writers on writing" are available in bookstores and libraries. You're bound to capture an idea or two from them.

Talk about writing. Making discussions about writing situations part of your daily routine will demystify the writing challenge, such as "writing this thing is impossible" or "I'll never be a good writer," and will replace negative thoughts with writing truths like "I'll get this writing job done" or "I can always improve my writing."

It is actually surprising that the workplace, where nonstop writing is such an important activity throughout the day, where the composing process is as important to the average employee as it is to authors, is also a place where writing is discussed so infrequently and so marginally. Take a moment to talk to teammates about what they do when they get stuck on a writing topic or what they did to succeed in an especially taxing writing task. Even if they answer, "I'm not sure," and you don't know how to respond to their vague answer, you are planting the seeds for further discussion about this critical issue. I often refer to certain organizations as *publication cultures*, a term that immediately resonates with those who have ever been in one. A publication culture is one in which staff constantly talk about the need for rough drafts, managerial review, and precise editing; where they use first-rate reference books and websites, where they receive writing training; where they look things up when disputes arise; and where they read high-quality literature from their field.

"Steal" ideas. I'm not encouraging criminal activity here. This is not a suggestion for violating copyright law. I am simply acknowledging that virtually every written work belonging to a company does not belong to the individual who wrote it, so you should feel free to employ its structure or quote a phrase or entire passage from it without fear of recrimination if it works for you. This rule also goes for you. When writing on behalf of the company, regardless of where, when, and on what you write, you may not claim ownership of the material. Copyright laws protect the company's right to ownership, unless you have a contract stating otherwise. Anyone from your job can use what you've written, provided it is used for approved company purposes. This being the case, why reinvent the wheel, recasting already acceptable text composed and edited by proficient writers?

Copying, or, if you prefer, modeling, is an excellent way to learn effective writing skills. In fact, one university professor, Leo Rockas, published an instructional resource, *A Creative Copybook*, with the premise that literal copying of excellent writing is a sure-fire means of tapping into one's own creativity. While you would be breaking copyright law by passing off material copyrighted by others as your own invention, the copying practice would be worthwhile, and it's certainly valuable when copying good writing by your own coworkers, including management.

FIGURE 4-1: Tips for Creating and Building a Writer's World

Environmental	Mental	Physical	Social
• Check lighting, temperature, ventilation, and noise levels. • Make ergonomic improvements. • Reduce clutter. • Surround yourself with beauty.	• Keep good reference books nearby. • Bookmark electronic resources. • Believe in yourself. • Count the number of words you produce. • Use the writing process.	• Keep a log. • Consider time of day. • Determine duration. • Improve typing speed. • Practice planning and drafting. • Eat, sleep, and exercise well. • Create a writing ritual.	• Hang around writers. • Talk about writing. • "Steal" ideas. • Make writing a lifelong activity.

Make writing a lifelong activity. Consider writing something you will always need to do both inside and outside work: in your formative years to write admissions essays for college and graduate school, during maternity leave to request that the insurance company reverse its decision on a non-covered medical procedure, in retirement to inquire about pension checks, at any time to write your travel agent or airline about a travel experience, and so on. This point means that you can make writing a whole-life activity, writing for your church group, community organization, school parents' association, co-op board, or whatever group you belong to. The more you write, the better you get at it.

Much of the writing you do outside work has applications to the writing you do at work. Take the case of a participant in one of my writing classes who said that she had never written a proposal for work but periodically writes one to foundations to endow her church group with a grant for a community program. Another participant said that she writes meeting minutes not at work but for her town library, where she serves as a trustee. If you can write a proposal for your church, then you can write one for your job; if you can write meeting minutes for your library, then you can write them for your job. Writing with a purpose applies to many facets of life. See the connections among them and deploy them as the need arises.

See Figure 4-1 for a review of the tips for creating and building a writer's world.

The Three Document Fixes That Will Dramatically Improve Your Writing

Moe: Now that I'm done with a draft, I'll spell-check.

Didi: Why would you want to do a thing like that?

Moe: I want to get it perfect.

Didi: Spell-checking is the last step to perfecting a draft.

Moe: Then what's the first?

Didi: The point—setting up the reader with the reason for reading it.

Moe: Why should that come first?

Didi: Because if it doesn't, you might be trying to perfect something neither you nor anyone else really needs.

Speedy Didi's point is so simple in its truth that its value could easily be overlooked. Think about someone you work with whose English is not so strong, maybe because she's still learning it or because he just lacks a formal education in the language. If you have had some sort of e-mail communication with such a person, chances are you have seen grammatical, punctuation, and spelling flaws. Let's say you received this e-mail from a coworker:

Hello,

No heat in office today. I call contractor to fix. He come but after check say he need relay switch, could take five day to get. I think we get other estimate because too cold. Please tell me and I do.
Irina

The use of language is clearly weak in those 5 sentences and 41 words. Nevertheless, Irina is still communicating what you need to know: The office is without heat, she called the designated heating contractor, the contractor diagnosed the problem, the problem is a faulty relay switch, the contractor needs five days to get the relay switch, the office will be too uncomfortable to work in for five days without heat, she thinks another contractor might solve the problem faster, and she wants your approval to proceed with a contractor search. What if Irina had written this:

Greetings,

I suppose that this is one of those times that try our souls. Much to the concern of the office staff, we are once again facing a deep chill, thanks in no small part to the faltering heating system, which seems to have a mind of its own. Knowing full well that this matter falls in your domain, I tried reaching you about this dilemma; however, as luck would have it, you were nowhere to be found. Thus, I took the liberty to contact the heating contractor. He was gracious enough to respond to my call immediately and arrive for a service call within the hour. I can see why you selected him. He's a very responsive gentleman, just the sort you would hope for in a critical situation. Unfortunately, however, his diagnosis of the problem and, more importantly, prognosis for a return to standard service, were not as expected. I would appreciate a call from you so that we can discuss this problem—sooner than later, hopefully.

Respectfully,

Irina

If you feel after reading those 9 sentences and 168 words that you were taken on a wild goose chase, a rhetorical dead end, who can blame you? Written in impeccable English, this second draft is clouded in ambiguous, purposeless chatter. If she wanted you simply to call, all she needed to write is, "We have an emergency here. Please call me." Now do you appreciate the first draft?

I am not trying to say that clear messages in substandard English are desirable, but I am insisting that fixing some problems in a message supersedes others in importance. I often hear people musing about how great it would be to get their messages done in one draft. The problem with that thinking is that it flies in the face of this simple truth:

Good writing is rewriting.

However, if you're hoping to make sense of just a quick look at your draft, you can prioritize rewriting tasks to maximize time efficiency. So, if you are now drafting quickly and want to check your message as quickly as possible before pressing send or print—in other words, if you want to reach your reader with maximum speed—read on to learn the rewriting step from the top down. You've just read all these useful tips for tapping into your inner psyche; now here's a practical approach for tapping into your readers.

After tearing through a draft, you could check it with the *5-minute fix, 10-minute fix,* or *20-minute fix,* depending on the time available, the value of the message, and the importance of the audience:

›   The 5-Minute Fix covers the highest-level issues—the big idea—that the reader needs addressed. During this first look, concern yourself with purposefulness and completeness.

›   The 10-Minute Fix covers the structural level, which helps the reader improve the focus on essential supporting points. Work on organization and format when giving your message a second look.

›   The 20-Minute Fix covers the ornamental level, the command-of-language issues that keep the readers tuned into your ideas and not obsessed by your linguistic hiccups. Attend to style when giving the message this final look.

When rewriting, you can use the analogy of building a house. First you need to decide the reason for the building (primary residence, vacation, rental, whatever) and the type of house (e.g., colonial, ranch, split level), and then you select the building materials; during the 5-Minute Fix, you determine the reason for the message and the contents to include. The builder then wants to ensure that the building will be structurally sound; in the same vein, the

10-Minute Fix focuses on the structure of the contents. Finally, the builder dresses up the house with all the appropriate appointments (garden, cabinetry, appliances, etc.); similarly, the 20-Minute Fix calls for elegance of expression, clarity and conciseness of sentences, and correctness of grammar, usage, and punctuation.

After tearing through a draft, you could check it with the 5-Minute Fix, the 10-Minute Fix, or the 20-Minute Fix (see Figure 4-2), depending on the time available, the value of the message, and the importance of the audience: *Where am I going?*, *When must I get there?*, and *How will I get there?* How can you start re-writing until you know your objective? To know what you want

FIGURE 4-2: The Three Document Fixes that Will
Dramatically Improve Your Writing

The Fix	The Task
5-Minute Fix: *Purposefulness and Completeness*	1. Assert your purpose statement in the opening sentence. 2. Separate the purpose from the rest of the document. 3. Check your closing for logical, useful next steps that connect to your purpose in the opening. 4. Review your supporting details against your plan. Add or delete ideas as you see fit based on your purpose and readers' concerns.
10-Minute Fix: *5-Minute Fix + Structure*	5. Limit paragraphs to one focused idea. 6. Lead each paragraph with the centralized point. 7. Employ a familiar organizational pattern for sentences following the lead sentence (e.g., most-to-least important, least-to-most important, general-to-specific, specific-to-general, chronology, cause-effect, advantages–disadvantages, or similarities–differences). 8. Use headings to separate big sections. 9. Use bullets or numbers to itemize points within a section. 10. Insert transitions to guide the reader from one idea to the next.
20-Minute Fix: *10-Minute Fix + Style*	11. Ensure that your tone is reader-sensitive. 12. Read the document aloud for correct sentence structure. 13. Edit sentences for clarity. 14. Eliminate verbiage. 15. Check grammar, punctuation, and mechanics (e.g., capitalization, abbreviation, number usage). 16. Check diction and spelling.

your reader to know or do is to answer the question *Where am I going?* You can't determine how much work you can put into a rewrite without knowing your deadline. So once you answer the second question, *When must I get there?*, you can determine whether you can deploy the 5-, 10-, or 20-Minute Fix, which, in effect, answers the third question, *How will I get there?*

The two case studies that follow should make clear these three fixes, which prioritize 16 qualities of a well-written business message.

Case Study 1: Speedy Didi to Mopey Moe

Situation: Didi is in a morning meeting with her manager and other company executives. She cannot leave but needs to contact Moe immediately about Project Now. She understands that, under tight time constraints, even the best writer needs to know when 90 percent good is good enough; therefore, she thumbs into her Black-Berry the following note to Moe: "Call me,"

Clearly, Didi has a tone problem (no *please* in her message), she made a punctuation error (a comma instead of a period), and she is not telling Moe why she needs to speak with him. Nevertheless, as her direct report, he probably would call her immediately, so she will achieve her objective. That's why getting to the point is so important—it puts the reader to work. Nevertheless, just before Didi presses the send button, she decides to put the message through the 5-Minute Fix:

The 5-Minute Fix: Purposefulness and Completeness

1. Assert your purpose statement in the opening sentence.
2. Separate the purpose from the rest of the document.

---

3. Check your closing for logical, useful next steps that connect to your purpose in the opening.
4. Review your supporting details against your plan. Add or delete ideas as you see fit based on your purpose and readers' concerns.

Didi takes the extra couple moments to address the point from her reader's point of view (purposefulness), and the supporting details (completeness), thus the 5-Minute Fix. This is what she now writes:

Call me before 3 p.m. today, about Project Now. We have a extra week, so I want to include the ilustrations after all. Lets come up with a solid plan for how to proceed. As a start, I'd like to include the Quito photographs and 2006–2007 sales comparisons. E-mail them to me for our discussion.

The message is still far from perfect. In fact, even more mistakes pop up. The tone is somewhat improved—except for those first and last pushy sentences. The comma after *today* needs to be deleted. The words *illustrations* and *Let's* are misspelled. The word before *extra* should be *an*, not *a*. Also, she has packed all her ideas in a single paragraph—never a good idea. Nevertheless, you have a clear set of expectations and a course of action. The 5-Minute Fix has been accomplished.

As the meeting ends earlier than expected, Didi realizes she has more time to rewrite the message—time for the 10-Minute Fix:

The 10-Minute Fix: The 5-Minute Fix + Structure

5. Limit paragraphs to one focused idea.
6. Lead each paragraph with the centralized point.
7. Employ a familiar organizational pattern for sentences following the lead sentence (e.g., most-to-least important, least-to-most important, general-to-specific, specific-to-general, chronology, cause-effect, advantages-disadvantages, similarities-differences).
8. Use headings to separate big sections.
9. Use bullets or numbers to itemize points within a section.
10. Insert transitions to guide the reader from one idea to the next.

Didi darts to her office and on her desktop computer rewrites through the 10-Minute Fix, the following message:

Call me before 3 p.m. today, about Project Now. We have a extra week so I want to include the ilustrations after all.

As a start, I'd like to include the following visuals:

- Quito photographs
- 2006–2007 sales comparisons

E-mail them to me for our discussion. Lets come up with a solid plan for how to proceed.

The small errors remain, but Didi has created a much clearer structure. The bullets plainly state what Moe needs to get to her before he calls. As a result of her improved structure, she places the closing thought where it belongs—at the end.

Before sending, Didi has a final thought: She might need to make more time for this message because several people at levels above, parallel to, and below her need to be copied. Now she works through the 20-Minute Fix:

The 20-Minute Fix: The 10-Minute Fix + Style

11. Ensure that your tone is reader-sensitive.
12. Read the document aloud for correct sentence structure.
13. Edit ideas for clarity.
14. Eliminate verbiage.
15. Check grammar, punctuation, and mechanics (capitalization, abbreviation, number usage).
16. Check diction and spelling.

With the luxury of a little more time, this is how Didi's message would look:

Please call me before 3 p.m. today about including illustrations in Project Now because we have an extra week.

Before calling, e-mail me the following visuals:

- Quito photographs
- 2006–2007 sales comparisons

> We'll include these and other illustrations once we devise a plan.
>
> Thanks,
>
> Didi

Notice how her conciseness has improved. The weak *I'd like to include* clause has been replaced by a more commanding *We'll include*. Yet Didi has a more polite tone-setting opening word (*Please*), as well as a gracious closing word (*Thanks*). Now she has improved the style, tone, grammar, and punctuation to go along with her strong attention to purposefulness, detail, and structure.

Of course, Didi could have fixed this limited example in 2 minutes, not 20, but these three fixes argue sensibly for the order in which we should rewrite our messages, depending on how much time we have. I've noticed a huge benefit to moving in the direction of the 5-, 10-, and 20-Minute Fixes: A lot of minor problems of grammar, punctuation, and spelling magically disappear anyway once you've taken care of purpose, completeness, and structure.

Now let's apply these fixes to a more involved message.

Case Study 2: Mopey Moe to Speedy Didi

Situation: After Moe responds to Didi's message in Case Study 1, he decides on a proposed approach to Project Now, which he wants her to consider for discussion during their 3:00 P.M. meeting. Returning to the template proposal in Figure 2-4 (see page 47), you can now see how his first draft looked, alongside the final draft (compare Figures 4-3 and 4-4).

FIGURE 4-3: Moe's Proposal, First Draft

The purpose of this message is to propose what I think to be a sound approach to completing Project Now on time and within budget. We could ask R&D to reassign Jane to recover some production time lost since she left the project. As you know, the problem is that Project Now is running behind schedule. Our project plan lists October 1 as the completion date for Phase 1. I believe that we have seven tests to run before we can move to Phase 2. We will not complete the project until December 14, two weeks past the projected completion date. Everyone involved in the project was planning the timeline for this project under the faulty assumption that at least three analysts would conduct the Phase 1 tests. Tom reassigned Jane to R&D on September 9. We have been able to complete only three tests a week. I spent some time coming up with some viable options. To complete the final seven tests, the remaining analysts told me some options, and I've come up with some ideas of my own, to get to within a week of the deadline. First, we could allow overtime. There's a lot of tough testing, and the extended working hours may compromise quality. Another option is to assign me to the testing team. I would have to suspend all my supervisory responsibilities if called upon to do so. Another thing we could do is reassign Jane to Project Now. This option would go a long way toward helping us to regain continuity and ensure that we've got enough coverage without ever sacrificing quality or supervision. I think we should return Jane to our group, which is our best option to gain at least a week of lost time. I would really appreciate your letting me know which way you want to go on this.

Step by step, this is how the document takes shape:

5-Minute Fix: Purposefulness and Completeness

1. Notice the big change in Moe's opening. His first sentence begins with the very action he wants Didi to take. This may seem pushy, but not to a thick-skinned manager who expects immediate solutions to pressing problems. In addition, he reduces the word count of the original two sentences from 43 words to a single sentence of 18 words.
2. He separates the purpose from the rest of the message in a paragraph of its own.
3. His closing statement is equally direct and separated from

FIGURE 4-4: Moe's Proposal, Final Draft

Asking R&D to reassign Jane to Project Now would recover some production time lost since she left the project.

Problem
Project Now is running behind schedule. Our project plan lists October 1 as the completion date for Phase 1, but we have seven tests to run before we can move to Phase 2. At this rate, we will not complete the project until December 14, two weeks past the projected completion date.

We planned the timeline for this project assuming three analysts would conduct the Phase 1 tests. Once Tom reassigned Jane to R&D on September 9, we were able to complete only three tests a week.

Options
I've estimated the time needed to complete the final seven tests and discussed with the remaining analysts three options to get to within a week of the deadline:

1. *Allow overtime.* Because of the painstaking level of testing, the extended working hours may compromise quality.
2. *Assign me to the testing team.* In this scenario, I would have to suspend all my supervisory responsibilities.
3. *Reassign Jane.* This option would help us regain continuity and ensure sufficient coverage without sacrificing quality or supervision.

Recommendation
Returning Jane is our best option to gain at least a week of lost time.

Please let me know how to proceed during our next project meeting.

---

the rest of the message. Also, it logically concludes his argument.

4. He eliminates unnecessary ideas like "I've come up with some ideas of my own" and "there's a lot of tough testing."

10-Minute Fix: Structure

5. Moe separates each supporting idea by paragraph.
6. Each of his paragraphs opens with the main point.
7. He uses the familiar organization pattern of problem-method-options-solution.
8. He inserts headings to separate the sections, allowing for easy scanning.
9. He lists the three options in numbered points to make them prominent for the reader.
10. He adds helpful transitions such as "At this rate" and "Once Tom reassigned Jane."

20-Minute Fix: Style

11. Moe moves from a wishy-washy tone to a focused, self-possessed one by eliminating phrases like "The purpose of this message," "I think," and "I would really appreciate."

At this point in the fixing process, Moe is just about done. The clarity, conciseness, grammatical correctness, and mechanics issues are minimal because he took care of the more important matters of purposefulness, completeness, and structure.

Speedy Didi must be smiling as she reads Moe's message. Under her patient and wise instruction, he has transformed from Mopey Moe to Mercurial Moe, a key player in WeCanDoIt Enterprises.

Applying the three fixes, as needed, to your lengthier proposals, reports, procedures, root-cause analyses, technical reviews, policy briefings, and white papers will make you faster. Use the checklist for the three fixes (Figure 4-2) the next time you're in rewriting mode—and you'll quickly begin seeing results.

CHAPTER

5

Health—Planning for the Unexpected

(*Moe and Didi discuss Project Now in her office. She waves his proposal.*)

Didi: This is a fine proposal, Moe.

Moe: Really?

Didi: You got it to me in time. It was to the point. I liked that opening summary statement. You gave me just what I needed to decide quickly, and you laid out the details for easy reference. The sentences were clear and concise. You nailed it.

Moe: Thanks. I learned it all from you.

Didi: Hey, you can lead a horse to water, but you can't make it drink. The credit goes to you.

Moe: So will you go with my recommendation: reassigning Jane?

Didi: I don't think I should. I've borrowed her services too often, and her department needs her desperately right now.

Moe: Oh.

Didi: I'm choosing Option 2. I'm asking you to do the extra work until the project is done, and I'll take care of whatever supervisory responsibilities of yours you need me to. This is the most cost-effective, politically right solution. We'll all have to roll up our sleeves now.

Moe: OK.

Didi: Sorry.

Moe: Don't be. I completely understand.

Didi: You do?

Moe: Like you said: You might not always agree with me, but you're depending on me to inform you thoroughly. I think you're saying that I gave you enough information to make a wise decision.

Didi: You sure did. Great job! (*Raises an imaginary glass.*) Here's to more of the same!

Moe: That's the thing. Just because I nailed it once doesn't mean I'll ever nail it again. How do I repeat this success?

Didi: Guess what? First, you hit this proposal out of the park. Second, you proved you had the right attitude when I chose an option other than the one you proposed. And now you want to know how to keep up the productivity and positive mindset. Brother, you have arrived!

Great question, Moe! This chapter is Didi's answer to Moe's question, "How do I repeat this success?" After achieving your speed-writing goals by trying the techniques described in the previous chapters of this book, how do you stay in the groove? Get back in the zone? Keep on the high road? Maintain those high standards you have been reaching? This chapter is all about sharpening your writing skills, believing in the strength of the system you've just established, knowing when and how to fine-tune it, working at it, going into any writing situation—no matter how challenging—with the confidence that you can get the job done.

Why use the word *health* for this leg of writing with *DASH*? Well, what do you need to deploy your good sense of direction, a remarkable knack for acceleration, and a towering source of strength? *Health*, obviously. Without that, you cannot keep doing what you set out to message after message, day after day, year after year.

While this chapter is about staying healthy to write faster and better, the opposite is true also: By writing, you can heal physically and emotionally. You can truly look at writing as a way of dealing with your health. Two essays by two great American writers come to mind. The first, "Sustained by Fiction While Facing Life's Facts," by Alice Hoffman, appeared in the *New York Times* (August 14, 2000). Hoffman had nursed a sister-in-law who succumbed to brain cancer and a mother who contracted breast cancer, all the while writing. But the challenge of her life came when she herself was diagnosed with breast cancer. Having survived ten months of chemotherapy, the author concludes, "Once I got to my desk, once I started writing, I still believed anything was possible." The other essay, by Amy Tan, "Family Ghosts Hoard Secrets That Bewitch the Living," also appeared in the *New York Times* (February 26, 2001). Tan recalls the life of her deceased mother, whose stories inspired Tan to write some of her own amazing tales. Attributing some of her success to her "ghostwriters" (her grandmother and mother), she reflects, "I found in memory and imagination what I had lost in grief." Writing, even writing at work, can be that cathartic, that revelatory. In a sense, it keeps us going.

Within Yourself—Dealing with Criticism and Feedback

To keep you going—to keep the state of your writing in the best of health—this chapter covers some best practices for cultivating a proactive plan to write under pressure and to plan as early as possible for time-consuming emergencies that might undermine your writing productivity. In the spirit of the George Harrison song "Within You Without You," you can look at staying healthy as a writer from two perspectives: within yourself and without yourself. That's what we'll cover here.

1. **Develop a thick skin**. Everything we write is a reflection of who we are, even if it also represents our organization's position. People are always judging us by what we write, presuming to know what we think and how we feel about the positions we are taking. Reflecting on this reality for any period of time could be enough to make us the worst sort of paranoid individuals imaginable. We have a choice here: to become neurotic about it and go into a shell of self-defeatism and intellectual atrophy or to let it fall off us like water, drink whatever worthwhile advice we can, and move on to the next important writing project. Too many people take criticism of their writing as criticism of their intellect, lifestyle, convictions, and values. Not so. You can be the greatest person in the world who just happened to write something that simply sucks. Get over your feelings and see what you can learn from the criticism. I have written numerous published works in a broad range of fields, and my wife has never published a sentence in her life. Nevertheless, her criticism of my writing—and she is by no means an expert

critic—is usually dead on. I listen, rewrite, and improve the essay or proposal or whatever it is I'm composing. How foolish I would be not to, as foolish as a builder who refuses to accept criticism when not laying a suitable foundation for a structure built on sandy soil or a surgeon who dismisses the guidance of life-support monitors hooked up to a patient. You should always take the attitude that the coworker or manager criticizing you is putting her own professional reputation on the line. As much is at stake for her as it is for you. She is giving you advice based on your own best interest, which is also her own best interest and, therefore, the company's.

And even if the person criticizing the writing has only ill will toward you—implausible as that may seem—or if the criticism is rendered crudely or viciously, you can still learn something from the criticism itself. Whether someone said, "You might consider rearranging that paragraph" or "Listen, scatterbrain, that paragraph is a jumbled mess," you still have gotten the same advice: fix that paragraph. Sure, you'd want to avoid the Neanderthal critic in the future, but don't be so quick to dismiss the advice.

Managers would be well advised to accept this attitude about writing criticism from subordinates. Speedy Didi would herself be a fool not to get input from subordinates—even a Mopey Moe—if she really wants to develop his skills and refine her own. I find as many managers as nonmanagers unaware of the stylistic decisions they make. Talking up this stuff makes everyone a better writer and reader.

To those people who say, "I can't stand that my manager always rewrites my drafts," I always answer, "As long as your manager keeps coming back to you for more drafts, why should you worry? You must be doing something right." Just worry the day your manager says, "We found someone else to write this one for us," because then you know your exit into professional oblivion is not far behind. You can't entirely control what others think of your writing, but you certainly can control how you take that criticism. Developing a positive approach to accepting feedback is indispensable for having a healthy mindset and improving your writing.

2. **Develop a system for constructive criticism.** This word of advice applies to your own writing as well as your coworkers'. Reviewing a teammate's writing by saying, "It's just wonderful, dear" is as useless as an inflatable raft on Mount Everest; by the same token, unleashing your fury with a relentless "This, that, and the other is awful" does little to guide the writer toward improvement. Find a way that summarizes both the strengths and the weaknesses of the writing and offer specific ways to improve the weaknesses *without* compromising the strengths.

My experience shows that writers who have a powerful sense of purpose may run into tone problems. Because they begin their messages with statements like "Here is what we have agreed to," "This is what I need you to do," or "You must send the following documents," their readers clearly know what they want, but they may find the tone unnecessarily demanding, demeaning, or demoralizing. The trick is to tone down the message without losing the clarity of purpose. Contrarily, some people graciously open without getting to the point with statements like "I have been thinking long and hard about your excellent suggestion," "After careful consideration of the situation in which we now find ourselves, I have meticulously pursued a course of action to determine the systemic cause of the problem," or "I hope that all is well with you and that you will take the proposal described in this e-mail in the spirit in which it was intended." These writers seem to have a lot of time on their hands. As long-winded as those statements sound, they are genuine attempts at appearing gracious and audience focused. But the trick is to get to the point without losing that reader-centered attitude.

In developing a system of constructive criticism, you should look for both the positive and the negative, in that order because you want the recommendations for improvement to follow the negative. Since people tend to avoid or tune out the negative, I suggest using my *A* & Q approach, with *A* standing for *appreciations* and Q standing for *questions*. Start by saying what you like about the writing. Examples might include, "Good job on getting to the point . . . The structure is rock solid . . . I like the way you expressed your reservations about the proposed plan . . . Your sentences are clear and concise . . . You show a strong command of language." Instead of telling the writer where she went wrong, try asking questions. If you think that the writer took too long to get to the point, you could ask, "Why did you delay the purpose statement until the very end?" Perhaps the writer will defend her decision, but more than likely she'll appreciate the fact that you telegraphed your difference of opinion on where it should be placed, and she will discover for herself the oversight. If the organization seems out of whack, you can ask, "Why did you place the history of the problem before the description of the problem?" The writer will see for himself that the reader needs the grounding on why the history is important and will likely reverse the order of these ideas. The critical point to keep in mind when giving feedback to others or yourself is to be as specific as possible.

A & Q works well because it respects the writer's intelligence. It doesn't seem as authoritarian to the recipient of the criticism as an outright "this works and this doesn't." Such criticism is nonsense anyway because, with writing being its subjective self, what might work for one reader might not work for another. If all writing could be applied to a mathematical model of criticism, then we would all be reading and rejecting the same books. The reality, however, is that what you like to read may not be what I like to read and vice versa. If you tell the writer the questions that remain for you as a reader, she can decide whether she wants or does not want to address those questions depending on who her audience is. I have tried the A & Q technique to great success in many of my workshops and have received extremely positive comments about this approach in participant course evaluations.

To get a glimpse of how the A & Q would work for a rough draft, imagine writing the letter in Figure 5-1 to your telephone company.

FIGURE 5-1: Letter for Critiquing, First Draft

Dear Representative:

I am writing for three reasons:

1. to inform you of my intention not to pay the late charge of $25.00 and finance charges of $17.39 noted on your recent bill because I did not receive a copy of your original bill
2. to authorize my husband, Frank Vella, to speak on my behalf about your bill since my job precludes me from calling you during the unreasonably limited hours that your customer service center is available
3. to express my disappointment that I had to wait 22 minutes (from 11:55 A.M. to 12:17 P.M.) today and make four calls during that time (I was disconnected the first three times) before finally reaching Vickie Towson, one of your representatives

Please resolve this matter with him expeditiously because I want to pay the final bill and end my patronage of a business that does little to keep its customers happy.

Sincerely,

Carmen Vella

I would provide feedback by saying, "Here's what I appreciate about your writing: You get to the point immediately with that succinct first sentence. You format the details in bullet points for easy reference. You make your expectation clear in that final sentence, leaving nothing to doubt." Then I would conclude with four questions to point the writer to places she can improve the message: "Do you want to come across as aggressively as you do? Will the sarcastic tone of that final sentence be useful in getting what you want? Are you sure you want to end your relationship with the company? Would an additional credit to your account as well as a reversal of the charges be just as satisfactory?"

Most serious writers would reflect carefully on these questions and give their draft a second look, especially after considering that final question. Serious writers also understand that no contradiction exists between being direct with your readers and respecting them; therefore, they will take the time to strike that balance in their opening. Finally, they will be careful in restricting their battles to ones they can win. Notice how in the second draft (see Figure 5-2) the third point is now in a paragraph away from the first two points because the customer service center has control over the first two points but only upper management has control over that final one. Why not focus readers on what they can manage? Finally, once the writer decides what she really wants, she decides to stick to those two points without asking for more than she feels a customer would be entitled to if she were providing the service. She now has a purposeful yet respectful, thorough yet concise message—all done during the 5-Minute Fix.

FIGURE 5-2: Letter for Critiquing, Second Draft

Dear Representative:

I have been having a difficult time trying to resolve some basic account management issues, so I hope that you can resolve them for me:

1. Reverse the late charge of $25.00 and finance charge of $17.39 noted on your recent bill because I did not receive a copy of your original bill.
2. Authorize my husband, Frank Vella, to speak on my behalf about future bills.

In addition, I would suggest that you extend the available hours to speak with a live representative in your customer service center as a way of backing your advertised commitment to quality customer care for those customers who work during your business hours. I had to wait 22 minutes (from 11:55 A.M. to 12:17 P.M.) today and make four calls during that time (I was disconnected the first three times), before finally reaching Vickie Towson, one of your representatives.

I look forward to your response and appreciate your efforts at resolving these issues.

Sincerely,

Carmen Vella

The A & Q criticism method is only one of several ways of providing feedback to writers. Perhaps you already have a great technique that you wouldn't trade for mine. Or maybe you use a couple of different techniques depending on whom you are giving the feedback to and then an entirely different technique when assessing your own writing. (As I do; I'm a lot more direct with myself.) If what you're using works, then keep using it; if trying the A & Q seems like a good way of looking at writing criticism, then try it. Continually assessing your method of critiquing your writing helps to keep a healthy approach to writing.

3. **Discover writing time**. "Lost time is never found again," Benjamin Franklin was fond of saying. Do a quick inventory of

times in which you cannot write, for instance when sleeping, walking, showering, cooking, eating with family and friends, exercising, shopping, gardening, driving, and attending meetings. By the time you add these minutes and hours to your day, the better part of 24 hours will have disappeared. Can you recapture any of this time to increase your available writing time (AWT)? On days that I drive 50 miles to locations in traffic-congested city locales, I say goodbye to between three and four hours of AWT; on the more frequent occasions that I take a bus or train to my appointments, I find additional AWT. And if I prefer not to write, I can always read and sleep, which are both essential for staying strong and healthy as a writer. Instead of driving yourself, try public transportation if it's available in your area. If that doesn't work, look for other opportunities to find AWT. You might skip one of those weekly lunches with friends to dine alone and write a half-dozen or so messages. You can pay someone to mow the lawn and use the found AWT to crank out a proposal. Get creative. Finding only ten minutes of extra AWT a day is equivalent to seizing *two full hours per month* from regular workdays. Finding AWT where you thought it wasn't is a great way to become a thief of time, a way to minimize the stress of always feeling you're trapped in a maddening rush from one deadline to another.

4. **Handwrite as little as possible if a computer is available**. Occasionally I hear writers (even famous and successful writers) say that they enjoy handwriting a first draft and then typing it. While I encourage all writers to write the way they prefer, I challenge them to prove to me that they can actually write faster that way. It's great that handwriting makes these authors feel good, but this book is about how to feel good when writing faster. People who have to write a lot at work write far more than the average famous writer. As proof, let's do the math. Compare what you

write at work to this book, which runs about 50,000 words. If you write about one message per hour the length of the one in Figure 5-2 (165 words) per eight-hour workday, you wouldn't be writing much. Really. Check your e-mails, reports, and other documents. I'm sure they would amount to more than 1,320 words per day. But using that low number and accounting for the average 240 workdays per year, you would be processing enough words to write five of these books every year—and that's a conservative number! Chances are you just don't have the time to handwrite everything before entering it on your computer. The computer is there to speed the writing process—use it.

5. **Make a record of the fires you have extinguished**. This practice is just plain good for your psyche because you'll always be reminded of your track record for getting things done. Here you are not just listing the writing chores you've finished but summarizing completed emergency writing projects—even minor emergencies. What follows is a list of fires extinguished compiled by Paul, an assistant manager at a commercial bank. The items listed are not part of his routine job description, so he considers each one an example of going above and beyond the call of duty.

> ▸ July 7: Proofread galleys for new employee orientation handbook.

> ▸ July 11: Wrote minutes for July 11 executive board meeting.

> ▸ July 15: Revised welcome letter to clients for Senior VP of Client Relationships.

> ▸ July 17: Researched money funds of Artists Bank and emerging mutual funds for CFO.

> ▸ July 23: Wrote monthly business review for July 25 executive board meeting.

You can imagine how long Speedy Didi's list of extinguished fires would run. Her every workday is an adventure in making the difficult look easy and the impossible seem doable. Each time she coached Moe she was putting out a fire, proactively managing situations before they became emergencies or successfully dealing with emergencies before they became crises. Her lists are more detailed, as she adds her completion time alongside each task. This is an example of an unusually busy workday, September 9:

›   Wrote first draft of Murphy proposal—30 minutes

›   Wrote final draft of Muhammad proposal—10 minutes

›   Created client file for project plan—15 minutes

›   Reviewed Moe's catastrophe contingency plan, wrote comments—15 minutes

›   Proofread team's section of annual report—5 minutes

›   Wrote first draft of article about new ventures for company newsletter—20 minutes

›   Outlined client needs assessment methodology for sales training module—30 minutes

From a practical angle, your notes on fires extinguished can serve as a blueprint for putting out the next fire, the next fast-paced writing assignment. Walking into writing tasks with a clear understanding of the Three Big Questions—*Where am I going?*, *When must I get there?*, and *How will I get there?*—will speed up the process and keep you focused. Keeping records of writing in a crunch helps you provide better estimates and maintain your sanity under pressure.

6. **Read writers on writing**. There are countless books on this subject. A good start would be the contemporary *Writers on Writ-*

ing: *Collected Essays from The New York Times, Volumes I* and *II* (2002–2004). Not all of the essays discuss the writing process, but they all feature insights into creativity by such contemporary writers as Russell Banks, E. L. Doctorow, Gail Godwin, Jamaica Kincaid, David Mamet, Walter Mosely, Joyce Carol Oates, John Updike, Kurt Vonnegut, Jr., and Alice Walker. Other valuable resources include *The Paris Review Interviews, Volumes I, II,* and *III* (2007–2008). The nearly 50 interviews in these books span a half-century of conversations with the world's most renowned writers, including Nobel Prize laureates Saul Bellow, T. S. Eliot, William Faulkner, Nadine Gordimer, Ernest Hemingway, Gabriel Garcia Marquez, Toni Morrison, Harold Pinter, and Isaac Bashevis Singer. All the interviewees discuss their approach to writing. While some of the commentary may seem idiosyncratic, all it takes is a quick read of different authors' writing routines to reinforce the idea that writing is work, and work requires a workmanship attitude. That attitude is their way of staying in shape as writers. We learn to write not by talking but by writing. All writers worth their salt say this.

7. **Read something inspirational**. A surefire way of overcoming writer's block is reading purposefully. Once the connection between reading and writing is made, writer's block ceases to exist. Writers need to read, plain and simple. Suppose you're stuck on an idea and you catch yourself staring blankly at the screen. Turning to a moment of purposeful reading could make the difference between wasting an hour and becoming a more informed writer.

By *purposeful* reading, I mean that the reading material should be related to the subject of the writing. If you're stuck while writing a proposal for a smartphone, doing an online search of "smartphone reviews" automatically gives you heaps of information to draw from. If you can't get past the opening paragraph of a requisition for office furnishings at a new location, then browsing a print or online catalogue would suffice for someone familiar with the topic; an online search for "furnishing an office" would be a great jumpstart for a less experienced writer.

Looking up reference material might not sound like the most inspirational activity in the world; however, turning to books or articles by admired writers on a variety of interesting topics is a great springboard to maintaining a regular writing regimen. Improved writing quality and productivity will follow as you learn to appreciate writers not just for the ideas they convey but for the way they artfully turn phrases, paint pictures with their words, build to climaxes, and respect the reader's imagination and intelligence. It will also raise the standard you set for yourself in an unthreatening way. In fact, it becomes as playful an approach to writing as does amateur sport when the weekend golfer pretends to be Tiger Woods or the occasional tennis player pretends to be Roger Federer. An example of how this might look on a large writing project follows.

Not long ago, I resolved to write an article on creativity, motivated by participants of my writing courses who over the years have asked the same question: "Can a person learn to become more creative?" I had no idea of the perspective I wanted to take or the point I wanted to make. After doing online searches on creativity and asking more knowledgeable friends what they knew about the topic, I began on my path of reading and writing in this general direction: I read quantum physicist David Bohm's esoteric book *On Creativity*, followed by Mihaly Csikszentmihalyi's more accessible bestsellers *Flow* and *Creativity*. At this point, the Bohm book seemed more practical than I had expected, so I went back to it to take notes. Getting some sort of grounding between the theoretical and the practical, I was ready to write a few comments based on a central point that had taken shape in my mind, namely that the creative mind makes connections between the apparently most divergent people, places, things, and ideas. I then turned to more practical ideas, some of which seemed helpful and others less so, from Tony Buzan and Barry Buzan's *The Mind Map Book*, Edward De Bono's *De Bono's Thinking Course* and *Parallel Thinking*, Michael J. Gelb's *How to Think Like Leonardo Da Vinci: Seven Steps to Genius Every Day*, and Daniel H. Pink's *A Whole New Mind: Why Right-Brainers Will Rule the Future*. Being a writer whose subject matter is often language itself, I returned to the topic of dialogue theory, which certainly demands a measure of creativity. This decision led me to Bohm's *On Dialogue*, Linda Ellinor and Glenna Gerard's *Dialogue: Rediscover the Transforming Power of Conversation*, William Isaacs's *Dialogue and the Art of Thinking Together*, and Daniel Yankelovich's *The Magic of Dialogue: Transforming Conflict into Cooperation*. Many more books followed, as my searches went from keywords of "creativity" and "dialogue" to "rhetorical theory," "randomness," "improvisation," and "thinking." I moved to books on the creative process by philosophers, teachers, composers, and authors. At this point, I was not reading from cover to cover but searching for ideas that would support or refute my positions, which kept taking shape as I took notes, which became sentences, which became crystallized ideas.

A note of caution here: I am not suggesting that you read as a means of escaping writing responsibilities. Remember that writing does not start until you write. Reading is not writing, thinking about writing is not writing, and even reading what you've written is not writing. Anything other than planning, drafting, and rewriting—the writing process described throughout this book—is just that: something other than writing. But what good is sitting there staring at a blank screen when you can be productive as a "mind miner," prospecting for ideas that can make you leap from the darkness of writer's block to the light of expression. See if jumping from writing to reading and back works for you. You will return to this practice again and again to promote writing productivity.

8. Befriend your writer's block. I have been spending a lot of space writing about ways to overcome writer's block because it is so common for many of us. Writer's block is pervasive because there are so many causes for it, such as possessing weak writing skills, having insufficient knowledge about the topic, taking criticism too much to heart, suffering from fatigue or stress, coping with environmental or physical blocks (as I mentioned in Chapter 4), and romanticizing what makes a good writer, among many others. I suppose, then, writer's block is inevitable from time to time.

If that's the truth, then here's an altogether different way of dealing with writer's block: Greet it, hang out with it, and get to know it—yes, befriend it. Here's how Mercurial Moe (he's no longer mopey) made writer's block his friend, not his enemy, with the help of Speedy Didi:

Moe: I try to make-believe writer's block doesn't exist.

Didi: Do you succeed?

Moe: No. It keeps telling me it does. And it's all over me now like the worst sort of leeches.

Didi: Seems pretty real to me. Is it a male or a female?

Moe: Huh?

Didi: What's its name?
(*Pause. Moe has an aha moment.*)

Moe: Ohhh. Jeannie.

Didi: Jeannie? As in Meany Jeannie?

Moe: You got it.

Didi: Make her comfortable. Ask her to sit down. You don't want her to go away too soon, or you'll never know why she came in the first place and when she expects to come again.

Moe: (*Playfully closes his eyes.*) OK. She's settling in.

Didi: How does she look?

Moe: Actually, pretty good looking.

Didi: It figures. She did up her hair and put on her best dress to impress you because she intends to stay a while.

Moe: She's more than welcome.

Didi: What are you going to say to her?

Moe: I'm not going to say anything. I'm just going to ask her a few questions, you know, get to know her a little better.

Didi: Sounds like a plan.

Moe: My first question is, "How intimidating do you really think you are?"

Didi: Boy, you're being forward!

Moe: Well, I'm a bit impatient with her.

Didi: Come on, Moe! This is the first time you met her. Lighten up. Let her get to know you, too.

Moe: I don't want her to like me to the point that she'll always hang around.

Didi: Aw, you don't know her well enough. You're letting her get the best of you already.

Moe: How do you figure?

Didi: If she likes you, then she can't hurt you. She preys only on people who are easily intimidated.

Moe: OK, I'll ask her what she likes so much about me.

Didi: Great question! What's her answer? (*He seems he's too embarrassed to answer.*) You know what? I think I'll leave you alone with her. (*She walks away as Moe carries on an imagined dialogue with Meany Jeannie.*)

Moe: What do you mean, I'm an easy target?

Jeannie: You're so quick to criticize yourself into a paralysis.

Moe: Why is that?

Jeannie: What do I care?

Moe: What gives you power over me?

Jeannie: I'm just here.

Moe: Well, do you mind sticking around while I write a few e-mails?

Jeannie: If you start writing, then there's no reason for me to stay.

Moe: Well, you're more than welcome to stick around. It's your choice. But I've got some writing to do. (*As he starts writing, Jeannie's intense stare transforms into a blank gaze and then to a distant glance, and she finally disappears as he hammers away at the keys.*)

Sounds ridiculous doesn't it? Not really. This approach to dealing with the pain of writing is no different from how physicians help patients cope with pain and psychotherapists counsel their patients to confront their anxieties, phobias, traumas, and demons. The best way to deal with pain, short of a miracle drug that eradicates it without altering your mental or emotional state, is to accept it, face it head on, understand it, and learn from it. Then you shall overcome, if not always at least to some improved measure of success.

9. **Burn down the icons**. The remarkable poet Grace Schulman, who has published six collections of her poetry and who happened to be one of my best college professors, wrote a brilliant poem called "Burn Down the Icons," which reminds me that we are flesh and not the human images represented in the sculptures, frescoes, and canvases found in museums and cathedrals, and our humanity makes us even more miraculous than any magnificent work of art. We should feel that way, too, when contrasting the writing we admire with the writing we actually do. Sure, we are taken by the beautifully turned phrase of a coworker with a strong command of language, and we would be remiss not to acknowledge the author's well-crafted sentence and masterful message. But we would also be foolish to blame ourselves for somehow constantly falling short of that high standard. Worse, we would be downright fools if we let some artificial model of excellence paralyze us and keep us from writing. Remember the admonitions in Chapter 1 about the myths of writing. Demystify it. You can still respect it without thinking it's some magical effort reserved for a chosen few. I am reminded of what the base-stealing legend Lou Brock said about what he called "base-running arrogance": As a baserunner, "You are a force, and you have to instill that you are a force to the opposition. You have to have utter confidence." So, too, must we feel about our writing. As Speedy Didi puts it, "I can get this done . . . it's just a bunch of words!" Icons aren't real except for the meaning we attach to them. We are real.

10. **Enjoy both the proactive planning and the reactive scheduling**. Since writing can be divided into steps, you can actually enter in your scheduler when you will plan, draft, and rewrite large writing projects. This practice will take care of the proactive plan-

ning part of scheduling. To deal with the reactive scheduling part, you have to be more flexible, understanding that schedules change because of shifting priorities, available information, and, often, serendipity. Getting stressed over inevitable moments such as these is simply wasted energy. Just plan those glitches forward!

11. **Accept and plan for inevitable emergencies.** Emergencies are a part of life. You can actually plan for them based on the type of environment you're in. How?

> ‣ Determine your peak writing times, and set them into your planner.

> ‣ Don't plan so many meetings when big documents are due.

> ‣ Plan to go to your e-mail at set times of the day, rather than react to each one as it comes in. If your job is to respond to e-mail, then try to handle each message as soon as you open it. This may seem a contradiction of what we saw in Chapter 3 about the Four Ds (*dump, delegate, defer,* and *do*), but it's not. If all you do is e-mail all day, then run through the Four Ds with each e-mail, but always with the objective of being done with it.

You are now equipped with a sharp mind, a can-do attitude, a writer's "arrogance," and a toolbox to handle yourself in pressure-packed writing situations. Now let's look at the people and problems that get in the way of deploying your best tactics for writing in a heartbeat. Let's move from within yourself to without yourself.

Without Yourself—Seeking Help from Others

Now that you've invested a lot of intellectual and emotional capital in yourself, it's time to invest it in others. Remarkable things happen when breaking away from our solitary selves; we realize our nature as social animals. To paraphrase the poet John Donne, "no writer is an island." While much of what we writers do is in isolation, we need the feedback and collaboration of others as a reality check of our ideas and a means for improving our style. With this mindset, review the suggestions that follow as ways of strengthening relationships to keep your writing fitness in top form.

12. **Take a walk around the office**. When you're struggling with a writing task for lack of information or just because you're justifiably tired of writing, get away from it all—even if for a few moments. Walk away from your workspace when you are getting eye- or arm-weary. Look around. Appreciate the presence of other people. Ask them what writing projects they're up to, without being a nuisance. Tell them what you're up to. Perhaps they have a suggestion or two to get you back in the writing trenches. If you have no one to talk to, then pick up the phone to achieve the same end.

I can't count the number of times such conversations produced for me an improved proposal, a more accurate or detailed report, or a new published article. One of my favorite questions is "What have you been reading?" especially when asking the many people in my life whose intelligence and insights I admire. The answer to that question often sends me on a long journey through new reading material that adds to my knowledge or entirely changes my outlook on an important issue. Of course, sometimes I don't take my friends' suggested reading advice because I'm facing tight deadlines or have other reading priorities or because the work in question doesn't suit my taste. Other times, I may take their recommendation, only to be disappointed by the material. But these cases are the rare exceptions. Mostly, I benefit tremendously on any number of levels: professional, intellectual, physical, social, spiritual. How amazing that the more one reads and learns, the more one sees how much more there is to read and learn! How can anyone traveling down this path ever be bored? The following lunchtime conversation between Speedy Didi and Mercurial Moe is just like many that have occurred in my life and in other writers':

Didi: What have you been reading lately?

Moe: Nothing much.

Didi: What's that book I always see you carrying in from your commute?

Moe: Oh. That.

Didi: Doesn't that count as reading?

Moe: I guess. It's just a hobby of mine.

Didi: What is?

Moe: Civil War stuff.

Didi: Oh? What are you reading?

Moe: Michael Shaara's *The Killer Angels*.

Didi: Great book!

Moe: You heard of it?

Didi: I read it.

Moe: You don't strike me as a Civil War buff.

Didi: I'm not really. I make a point of reading all the Pulitzer Prize–winning novels.

Moe: And for me, it's the opposite. I'm not too much into novels. I like nonfiction accounts of the Civil War. I read every Bruce

Catton book on the Civil War, and my favorite is James Mc-Pherson's *Battle Cry of Freedom*.

Didi: I have Shelby Foote's huge narrative trilogy on the Civil War.

Moe: Wow! Did you like them?

Didi: I doubt I'll read them. They were given to me as a gift. You want them?

Moe: To borrow maybe. I've always wanted to read his southern slant on the Civil War.

Didi: You can have them.

Moe: Really?

Didi: Not a problem. I'll bring them in tomorrow. You'd be doing me a favor. They take up a lot of space.

Moe: Don't you just hate that! A relative gave me this huge book—more than a thousand pages—by a writer named Joan Didion.

Didi: I love her! I read her novels, and they were all great.

Moe: I'm going to end up chucking it.

Didi: Is it called *We Tell Ourselves Stories in Order to Live?*

Moe: Yeah, that's it.

Didi: That's her collected nonfiction. I want that book! I can use it as a reference for a graduate course I'm taking.

Moe: You can have it. That's the least I can do for the Shelby Foote books.

Didi: That's a deal.

Moe: You bet.

You've heard the expression "One person's trash is another person's treasure." Sharing resources is just one benefit of communicating with people about what they're reading. The ultimate benefit is learning new ideas that might make your job easier or even improve your life. I owe a lot of my career to people who shared something they knew that I did not.

The same goes for writing material:

Moe: Do you have any completed audit reports?

Didi: I'm sure we do in the Internal Affairs group. I could show you an audit report of our group. Why do you need it?

Moe: I thought that would be a good approach for reviewing some of our operational problems. (*Hands her a document.*) This is one that I used in my old job.

Didi: (*Reads it quickly.*) Wow! This one is better than ours! Why don't you use this one?

Access to a lot of great workplace documents can be gathered through quick chats. Once those conversations flow, libraries of documents begin to appear. Before you know it, you'll be the bona fide source of company or department information.

13. **Establish clear deadlines**. Put deadlines in writing. If they're not in writing, they're not going to happen. Amazing things happen when you commit them to paper. They become real. To make and meet your deadlines successfully and to improve when you don't live up to your own expectations, consider these ten tips on successfully meeting deadlines:

Tip 1: Be specific. Don't write, "August—complete Donald Duck Report." Don't even write, "Week of August 24. . . ." Give a specific date, even a time. That's what it takes to get into the habit of committing yourself. Write, "August 24, noon—complete

Donald Duck Report." The exact deadline gives you a concrete objective, and it makes meeting the objective all the more enjoyable.

Tip 2: Be realistic. Don't pressure yourself unnecessarily. In fact, if you're new at setting deadlines, think the opposite. Set ridiculously reachable deadlines. If you know a status report takes you 15 minutes to complete and you have all of today free, set the deadline for tomorrow at 4:00 P.M. You want to set yourself up for success, not failure. As you get better at meeting these deadlines, you can begin squeezing yourself a bit more by tightening the deadlines.

Tip 3: Be responsible. Once you set the deadline, take it seriously. You've already given yourself plenty of time to complete the writing task; now use that time to get it done. There are no excuses. Make your word mean something to yourself.

Tip 4: Be diligent. Work. Decide whether the writing task is a free, formulaic, or fresh one. Always ask the Three Big Questions: *Where am I going?*, *When must I get there?*, and *How will I get there?* Think through the Four Ds when intrusive e-mails and phone calls arrive. Use the planning techniques described in Chapter 2 and the drafting approaches noted in Chapter 3. Rewrite with the 5-Minute, 10-Minute, or 20-Minute Fix, depending on the time you've allotted yourself. Keep the wheels spinning. If your boss says the writing assignment is due tomorrow, lie to yourself—make it due today!

Tip 5: Be alert. Look for unexpected moments of free time, that seemingly interminable moment when you're waiting in an endless line at the bank, or no one but you has shown up for the meeting on time, or you're at the car dealership waiting for an oil change, or you're in the waiting room for a medical appointment. Time is there waiting to be found. Use it to write. Remember that you're just writing a bunch of words, words that get produced with each passing moment that you write them.

Tip 6: Be forgiving. If you don't meet a deadline or two, don't self-flagellate. Get over it. Nobody's perfect. You'll make the next deadline.

Tip 7: Be critical. There's a flip side to this coin. Don't forget to learn something from the missed deadline. A missed deadline could be the greatest gift you've ever given yourself as a writer. Think about it. The cause behind that setback could be your entire problem in a nutshell. Perhaps you're setting unrealistic deadlines, biting off more than you can chew, goofing off too much, depending too much on others for their share of the writing task (more about collaborative writing later), or being weak at one step of the writing process. Don't just let the moment pass. Figure out why it happened and what you can do to prevent its recurrence.

Tip 8: Be flexible. If you have to reset a deadline occasionally, big deal. Life happens. Just change the deadline and timeline, making sure that you clearly inform whoever is waiting on you about the inevitable schedule change. I would hate to do this myself; I have never missed a writing deadline in my life. I have been up until 4:00 A.M. with a 5:00 A.M. wake-up call to meet deadlines, but, because of this attitude and, admittedly, obsessive scheduling, I don't break commitments.

Tip 9: Be congratulatory. Keeping commitments brings me to the next invaluable point: Pat yourself on the back when you hit those deadlines. Go ahead. Don't worry; no one's listening. Say to yourself, "There I go again! I'm great! I can do it! Nothing can stop me! Bring it on, baby! I'm fearless!" You can't help smiling when you say that, can you? Maybe no one can hear you when you're saying that to yourself, but everyone sure can see that exuberance and confidence bursting forth, that aura of invincibility. It not only feeds on itself; it's infectious. People will see you as the go-to person on this or that writing project, you'll be invited in for others, and you'll become a better writer all the time.

Tip 10: Be proactive. You call the shots. Be in charge to the extent that you can. Without being a pain in people's necks, try to steer deadlines to suit your schedule, and avoid sounding arrogant about it. Having as much control as possible over things makes it much easier for you to let go of the control when called upon—a much-needed ability for becoming flexible and avoiding becoming a control freak.

14. Set clear expectations with managers and collaborators. Be honest about your ability and your coworkers' ability to actually meet the established deadline. If you need more time, say so. If you don't have it, see if you can cut a corner or get help. If you can't, go for it!

There are two other huge aspects to setting clear expectations: the time-management skills of your collaborators and the demands of your managers. They alone can be the cause of your feeling pressured with writing assignments. First, take ownership of the problem yourself, and always be willing to accept 51 percent of the responsibility for the time pressures and missed deadlines, even when you're 100 percent innocent. With that mindset, let's look at collaborators and managers one at a time.

Collaborators. These folks are your peers, subordinates, superiors, vendors, or clients. Be open with them. Say you have a report that requires you to collaborate. Explain to your partners how important meeting the deadline is to you. Tell them what you're willing to do to get this job done, and, after making your task seem twice as hard as theirs, ask if they can meet their end of the bargain. Does this advice pertain to clients? Especially! You owe your livelihood to them. They're the ones you definitely want to come through for, so they need to be educated on what it takes to get the writing job done as scheduled. Here is how Speedy Didi might handle Mercurial Moe on a shared project.

Didi: (*Hands Moe a sheet of paper.*) Here's the outline of a new marketing report we have to complete for a Friday morning meeting with senior management. It took me a long time and a lot of sweat to come up with this plan.

Moe: (*Reads it.*) So you'll do the executive summary, introduction, and conclusion, and I'll do the statement of problem, methodology, and analysis?

Didi: Yeah. That will put most of the pressure on me because I can't get started until you finish your part. And I have to have a couple meetings with the CFO and COO to see what their objectives are.

Moe: Would that affect what I have to write?

Didi: Not at all. You just write; I'll spin it as needed.

Moe: When do you need it by?

Didi: Well, today's already shot. That gives us only Wednesday and Thursday. I'll tell you what: If you get your piece to me by Thursday at 3:00, I'll stay here late into the night and finish the rest of it.

Moe: Today's not entirely shot. I'll get started on it now. I don't want to give it to you at the last moment, just in case you need me to make changes and because I don't want to put all that pressure on you.

Didi: Hey, what else is new? But all the better if you can get it to me sooner.

Moe: Not a problem.

A lot is going on there. Didi is giving Moe all the respect in the world, but she's still turning the screws on him by saying that she's putting herself under a lot of pressure by giving him until the last minute to do the job. Without asking, she's gotten him to commit to an earlier deadline, one she knows he can meet. And even if he can't meet it, she has already cleared her schedule to work late on Thursday to get the job done if necessary.

Try some of these approaches yourself when collaborating. Be fair to yourself, but by all means try to get your collaborators to commit to their deadlines.

Managers. This is a source of greatest concern for most writers at the office. They complain about their managers' unrealistic deadlines, unclear instructions, insufficient guidance, or callous dispositions. These attitudes are a far cry from the Speedy Didi school of management, but even she needs managing if you're Mercurial Moe. In the previous scenario, suppose Moe's already facing a number of deadlines and he knows that he cannot meet them all. He needs to negotiate right there and then. He cannot expect Didi to read his mind and discover when the deadline passes that he was too overworked to get the job done. The deadline remains his responsibility. Their dialogue continues:

Moe: You know that I'm also working on the Biosphere Report and the Calgary Proposal, right?

Didi: Yeah. How are they going?

Moe: One's slower than the other.

Didi: When are they due?

Moe: You said they're due Thursday, too, and you gave them to me just yesterday and today.

Didi: Well, I need the Biosphere Report for the same meeting no matter what.

Moe: Can Calgary wait until Friday?

Didi: If anything must, then Calgary can.

Moe: OK. Marketing and Biosphere reports by Thursday; Calgary by Friday.

Moe has a trick or two up his sleeve as well. He knows he's likely to get all three writing projects done on time, but he has given himself an escape clause on one of them in the event that he falls behind. Also, he controlled the conversation in such a way as to get his manager to make the decisions and to commit herself to them.

If you can achieve this kind of buy-in from your manager, you will feel a lot more in control when you go back to your desk, confident in the knowledge that you have your boss's support. You will also reap a far greater benefit: a reputation for having a professional ethos that is hard to match.

15. **Keep asking**. Even when you think you've arrived as an efficient writer, keep asking for feedback on your writing. If your boss tells you that she's seen improvements in your writing, ask her in what areas. Is it your purposefulness? attention to detail? tone? organization? clarity? conciseness? Don't miss an opportunity to have your writing evaluated. Just for the asking, your writing will improve, and with the improvement will come improved turnaround time.

Also, remember to ask for areas where improvement is still warranted. Are you sensitive to your audience's concerns? Are you making any grammatical errors? Could the word choice be better? Is there a punctuation weakness? Is your production time satisfactory? We all need to improve our writing—even Speedy Didi. By asking relentlessly, you will let your manager or collaborators know that you mean business. In fact, you will make them better at what they do by asking them for the critique!

16. **Take nothing for granted**. One closing observation for maintaining your writing health: Assume that things will go wrong all the time. Trains can break down or run late. Traffic jams can keep you in your car for an hour longer than you anticipated. Managers can change their mind about what they want in your document. Medical emergencies can send you or a collaborator home or to the hospital. Need I go on? As I said earlier, life happens. You need to work with people while accepting the ever-evolving, unpredictable current of life. Many years of not missing a deadline has taught me one thing: not that I will make the next one, but that the percentages are against my keeping that record perfect. Do whatever you can—especially communicate with others—to deal with the ebb and flow of humanity. Stay healthy.

Now you are good to go, Moe!

6

DASH—Keeping a Fresh Approach

Moe: Thanks, Didi.

Didi: For what?

Moe: For everything. Your patience. The writing tips. Your confidence in me. The whole darn thing.

Didi: It's all back to you, Moe.

Moe: I wouldn't have improved without you.

Didi: Hey, if I take credit for when you do well, I'll have to take blame for when you mess up. Believe me: It all goes back to you.

Moe: (*Points to his head.*) So how do I keep all this up?

Didi: You will.

Moe: I already notice that I write better when you're around, and when you're not I slip.

Didi: Then I'll send you a picture of myself staring right at you for when I'm not around. That'll keep you honest.

Obviously, Speedy Didi is kidding. What she's really saying is that Mercurial Moe should write everything at work as if it were for his boss because, in fact, it is. Everything we write on the job or on our business's computers, handhelds, or other equipment, no matter where we are or when we're writing, is the responsibility of the company; therefore, we need to be vigilant about how we conduct ourselves when writing. Moe needs to employ the best practices for writing in a heartbeat described in this book because they will help him achieve a consistently efficient level of production.

Achieving such professionalism is no small task in light of the fact that many of us work all weekend long in our homes or in airport terminals, restaurants, and public conveyances. Our 24-7 accessibility via our smartphones adds additional pressures on writing quickly at a high professional level. The writing demands on us are unprecedented.

This reality is actually good news for our writing development because it makes writing a lifelong activity by giving us continuous practice. The operative word here is *practice*. Plying any trade requires regular practice. Once you're out of practice for a while, you lose touch with the fine points, the subtleties, of your discipline. Ask any surgeon, medicine man, carpenter, or faith healer, and they'll corroborate this position. So, as you begin plying your trade of writing in a heartbeat, you might want to summon everything you read here. That's what this chapter is about: reviewing what we've discussed so you could write with *DASH*—direction, acceleration, strength, and health.

Writing with Attitude

I love the irony of that Alan Jay Lerner and Frederick Loewe song from the musical *Brigadoon*, "Almost Like Being in Love." Tommy, the character who sings this song, sums up his feelings about Fiona by proclaiming, "Why, it's almost like being in love." But he completely supersedes that self-parodying hedge by what he sings before that refrain: "There's a smile on my face for the whole human race . . . All the music of life seems to be like a bell that is ringing for me." Clearly, he's madly in love.

Forgive the analogy, but you when you write at work, you are a writer, and if what it takes to write well and fast is to feel "almost like being a writer," then let this summary chapter help you feel that way. This book opened with the various situations (solo writing, team writing, and writing for the boss's signature) and environments (the office, home, crowded public places) in which you might find yourself as a business or technical writer. The demands for writing well and then delivering more of the same time and again will not cease, so you have read this book for a practical approach to writing fast under pressure. You've read about the need to have the right attitude about writing. You might recall the contrasting attitudes of Speedy Didi and Mopey Moe in Figure 1-1. Speedy Didi is a winner because she understands what amounts to a confidence game, the self-fulfilling prophecy that if you think you can't get it done you can't, and if you know you can you always will. You have learned what it takes to succeed, and maybe you've started to try those practices, adapting them to fit your skills, temperament, writing tasks, and goals. This means effectively using your writing tools—your desktop and laptop computers, smartphone, tape recorder, and old-fashioned notebook. But do the math. If one means is faster than the other, then use that one, not the other.

Here is a summary of the key takeaways of *How to Write Fast Under Pressure.*

1. **Destroy writing myths and hold fast to writing realities.** Surrender every excuse. No "I don't have the time" or "this is too much to get done" allowed. For those who think their excuses are legitimate, I strongly recommend reading the book *The Diving Bell and the Butterfly* by Jean-Dominique Bauby, who was the editor-in-chief of *Elle*, one of the most famous fashion magazines in the world. At the age of 43, Bauby had a stroke that left him in "locked-in syndrome," giving him the ability to move only his left eye. By blinking his left eye, one blink for *yes* and two blinks for *no*, he dictated to an assistant a 140-page book, letter by letter, and he survived until it was published, passing away two days later. His unsentimental account of his life was made into a movie by internationally renowned artist and filmmaker Julian Schnabel. I highly recommend both the book and movie. Anyone experiencing doubts about his or her writing will immediately run out of excuses for not writing after reading Bauby's book or viewing the movie based on the book. Remember that dwelling on the myths erodes writing time, whereas maintaining a mindset grounded on writing realities keeps you on task.

2. **Reflect on your treats and tricks to keep motivated.** Always keep at the forefront of your mind what has gotten you this far. What have you already accomplished as a writer? The answer "nothing" is also not allowed. We're not looking for bestselling books or thousand-page dissertations. Think small: the e-mail that immediately alerted someone to a problem, the weekly update or monthly status reports that you've submitted on time but that everyone, including you, has taken for granted. Contemplate not only the treat of having accomplished the task as scheduled but the trick you turned to make it happen. Those tricks are many, so

track the ones that work for you. Committing to a written plan, finding protected writing time, getting into the office a half-hour early, using the writing process efficiently, tuning out the incoming phone calls and e-mails—all of these and many more have worked for me and, undoubtedly, for you. Pull out those tricks when you need them.

3. **Remember DASH—direction, acceleration, strength, and health**. Embedded in these four necessary ingredients for success in athletic and artistic endeavors are loads of ideas for keeping in peak condition regardless of the message you write, the people you write for or to, and the places or times in which you write. Living *DASH* means never having to worry about writing. I spent a good part of Chapters 1 and 2 giving you plenty of reasons for fearing the prospect of writing. It is the hardest of the communication skills, much harder than listening, speaking, and reading. We are forever balancing the creative and critical sides of writing (see Figure 2-1) without receiving immediate feedback and without really knowing how our readers will accept our message. That said, we still have to do it—which brings us to this next point.

4. **Understand the writing process**. The three steps of the writing process are planning, drafting, and rewriting. When planning, we are brainstorming and organizing ideas not just in our head but on the screen or on paper. Chapter 2 focused on seven planning techniques, what we call idea generators, to break through writer's block: *can it* (boilerplate), *set it* (templates), *ask it* (preset questionnaires), *scoop it* (a summary or purpose statement), *chart it* (mapping), *post it* (movable notes), and *list it* (outlining). Using the right IG in a given situation can make a difference in whether you'll hit the ground writing on a time-sensitive writing project.

When drafting, we are writing what amounts to a review copy

with an SUV focus—speed, uniformity, and volume. We eschew quality in favor of getting to the end quickly and writing as much content as we can, staying reasonably close to the assigned topic. Two drafting techniques described in Chapter 3 are *free-writing* (using stream-of-consciousness in composing sentences) and *dialoguing* (writing down the most important questions or assertions specific audience members would have about your topic and answering them in dialogue form). Some free-writing practice suggestions appear in Figure 3-3. When rewriting, we shift our attention to quality. At this time, we deploy the 5-Minute Fix (purposefulness and completeness), 10-Minute Fix (structure), or 20-Minute Fix (style) to improve our final draft, depending on the time we have at our disposal. This hierarchical procedure of revising and editing includes 16 steps, all listed in Chapter 4.

5. **Know how to work the writing process to your benefit.** We all deal with three levels of writing complexity at work: the *free*, the *formulaic*, and the *fresh*. The free level is so easy that it requires little more than the drafting step of the writing process. Routine reminders and responses are examples. The formulaic level includes documents that more or less follow an established format. Since a template has been given to us, the planning step is already done; however, the document is important enough to merit careful writing; thus, we must rewrite as well as draft. Falling into this category might be staff evaluations, status reports, and meeting minutes. The most challenging writing is at the fresh level, where we may be struggling with an appropriate opening or grasping for the right amount of detail. In these cases, the entire writing process becomes vital to speeding up the writing chore. Figure 3-1 shows how these levels of complexity coincide with the writing process. Applying this knowledge to your own writing tasks will give a boost to your ability to get started with confidence.

6. **Ask the Three Big Questions.** Chapter 2 concludes with a detailing of the Three Big Questions—*Where am I going?, When must I get there?*, and *How will I get there?* Whenever a mess of writing projects has put your back against the wall, answering these questions will go a long way to getting you back on track. The first two questions provide a sense of purpose and direction, creating an urgency crucial to getting the job done on time. The last question impels us to face the reality of what to include and exclude from the document—as well as how much of the writing process is necessary for the writing task. As I write these words for the first draft of this book, I have answered the Three Big Questions:

> ‣ *Where am I going?* To the end of this book with this chapter.

> ‣ *When must I get there?* Today at 6:00 P.M. (It is now 9:00 P.M. on December 30).

> ‣ *How will I get there?* By summarizing the key and unique points from each chapter that I want my readers to remember to write in a heartbeat.

Try answering the Three Big Questions on the smallest of writing assignments (e.g., meeting reminders, routine requests, lab results), and then work your way up to longer, more challenging writing tasks. I'm sure you'll be pleased with the results.

7. **Work through the Four Ds.** Once you're in a writer's zone, the last thing you want is an interruption. Unfortunately, dealing with interruptions is a necessary part of most people's jobs. Those e-mails can be the most time-consuming interrupters because they may require time to write back, and, as we have already seen, writing is the slowest of the communication skills for most people. This is the moment when you can make great use of the Four Ds: *dump, delegate, defer*, and *do*. Your first choice is to dump it (by

deleting the e-mail or filing it without performing more than a keystroke or two). If you can't say yes to dumping the e-mail, then see if you can delegate it to someone else by forwarding it. Your next alternative is to defer the response to a specific time when you will be free of your present writing task. Finally, if all else fails, do it as quickly as you can, remembering to answer the Three Big Questions and to apply the writing process to the appropriate level of writing complexity. Chapter 3 provides an in-depth case study of how Speedy Didi used the Four Ds to tear through her writing assignments.

8. **Resist the common energy stoppers**. Chapter 3 looked at four ways we sabotage our writing productivity: having no plan when we need one, trying to complete all the steps of the writing process simultaneously, making of the message more than it really is, and worrying unnecessarily. Again, employing the writing process is a deterrent to these problems. Having faith in its steps and balancing their creative and critical elements by using both sides of your amazingly fertile brain will help you overcome these time-wasters.

9. **Build a writer's world.** Once we went through the technical aspects of planning and drafting, it seemed urgent to uncover ways to get ourselves under control before we could get our documents under control. For this reason, I mentioned 20 tips (see Figure 4-1) before delving into the three document fixes at the end of Chapter 4. Taking these tips to heart and using them to build a strong writer's mind and body must precede quality rewriting. I often teach the rewriting process to some people who use it to great effect, while others sitting alongside them can't make much of it in improving their messages. Some people are just more ready than others—but why? I reckon they're just stronger writers. To be in the same peak condition as the strong ones, read the section called "Building a Writer's World," in Chapter 4, which covers

four domains: our environmental, mental, physical, and social states.

Environmental issues include checking lighting, temperature, ventilation, and noise levels to promote writing efficiency. Making ergonomic improvements can contribute to your comfort, especially since writing often requires prolonged periods of being sedentary. The three general areas of ergonomics are physical, cognitive, and organizational, some of which are more in the writer's control than others. Additionally, reducing clutter has a great effect on clearing up the cobwebs in your mind that lead to unclear thinking when you're writing. Finally, surrounding yourself with beautiful objects, great art, and inspiring images and quotations helps to bring control to your environment, creating a greater sense of responsibility when writing.

Among the mental issues that you can bring to bear in making a stronger writer's world are the reference books and online resources you keep nearby, such as dictionaries, thesauruses, style books, and other industry-specific materials. But all of the reference resources and technical skills in the world are useless without a deep belief in your ability to get the writing job done. Word counting is a device that many successful writers use as a means of tracking their productivity and their progress. Also, keeping strong mentally depends on using the writing process illustrated in this book. Knowing that the process is done in steps gives you the opportunity to plan writing jobs in stages, according to when you expect to plan, draft, and rewrite.

Anything that keeps your body connected to the writing task figures as a physical issue. While keeping a log affords the great benefits of tapping into the intellect and storing ideas for future reference, its physical benefits should not be overlooked. Taking notes about events experienced and recording ideas are actually ways of staying in shape, keeping clear the cognitive pathway between your brain and your hands. Working at the time of day that's right for you and for clearly defined time frames is also helpful in reckoning with your endurance level. Since final drafts always end up on the computer these days, improving your typing speed—if improvement is needed—will yield big rewards in terms of productivity. So will practicing the planning and drafting steps of the writing process by using the techniques mentioned in Chapters 2 and 3, because those steps are usually the most time-consuming moments of composing. Other basic health issues also apply: eating, sleeping, and exercising well. In addition, ritualizing the writing experience is common practice among many successful writers. Whatever the ritual you might create, notice if it helps you feel more at ease when writing. If it does, keep doing it; if the benefit fades, add something new to the ritual.

The final domain in which you can reach your best self is the social. Hanging around writers, if you know any, is an invaluable asset as you develop your writing skills. Find out about the practices and proclivities that make them tick as writers; most of them will be flattered you asked. After you learn what they do, do it yourself. It might work. If you can't find a writer, read what writers have written or said in interviews about writing. You can also talk about writing to your teammates and managers. Here I'm talking about writing qua writing, not only the finished product of writing, although that's a big help, too. Knowing that most writers face the same problems you do when composing gives you more than a heartened feeling; it's informative in making you more capable of writing on demand. Since all the writing you do at work belongs to the organization you represent, why not be an idea thief, as well? Following the lead of writers you respect at work is essential. If I were new to an organization, the first thing I would do before writing an assigned document is to ask if there are models I can follow. I would want to conform to the company's expectations and style. Once I've copied a few, I'm ready to write my own documents without assistance, just like a kid moving away from needing the training wheels on his bicycle. Making writing as common an activity as eating, doing the dishes, or singing in the shower serves as a closing point to reaching yourself. Take friends along to writers' interviews, to book discussions, and to other literary events. Volunteer to write for your church or temple, or for your community, parents', or homeowners' association. Write to family members and friends whenever you can. Through countless social networking activities, just become the writer you have to be to write fast at work.

Making It Last

Another way of looking at Chapter 5 is to recall the adage "If you don't use it, you lose it." We gave the idea of staying healthy a 360-degree look: the literal as well as the figurative, the visceral as well as the intellectual, the physical as well as the spiritual. As such, we had many ways of looking at making our newfound skills real, putting them to good use, and making them endure over the long haul. We saw how inward and outward reflection on our connection to writing would inspire, fuel, and sustain us.

We started with this admonition: *Develop a thick skin.* We are always being judged, just as we are always judging everybody else, so get over the criticism, whether it's unadulterated praise or a philippic. Those of us who claim not to be judgmental forget we are being just that when we call other people judgmental or when we state whether we liked or didn't like a book we read, movie we saw, or song we heard. Expecting to be exempt from criticism is absurd. Go out of your way. Seek criticism. Know that it's coming. Accept it in the spirit in which it's intended—to improve your writing and the organization's message.

175

While we're on the subject of criticism, create a valid, reliable system for writing criticism. Consider using my A & Q style (appreciations and questions) and commit to memory the 16 elements of the 5-Minute Fix, 10-Minute Fix, and 20-Minute Fix. They're time-tested and highly effective, not only in my hands but in the hands of many people I've trained in writing assessment over the years.

Always look for free time. It's there more than you'd think. Take an available writing time inventory, and see where and when you can squeeze in a few more minutes. Once you're in writing mode, use the fastest tools available to you. That means preferring the computer to paper when deadlines are looming.

Record your own writing successes, the fires you have extinguished, and even your treats and tricks. Keeping a track record of your writing accomplishments when you had to meet big deadlines is a way of validating your writing ability.

Read what professional writers have to say about their own writing and writing in general in any number of books and articles on the topic. And if you're not inclined to reading writers, read something inspirational—whatever it is. Remember that to become a good writer, you have to read and write a lot. There are no shortcuts to this advice. Make reading a routine part of your life.

If you still get writer's block, laugh at it. Make it your buddy. Get to know it. Even if the thought of becoming friendly with writer's block is abhorrent to you, remember the famous line that Michael Corleone recalls learning from his father in *The Godfather*: "Keep your friends close but your enemies closer." Get to know what makes your writer's block tick, and deal with it accordingly. Once you humanize it, you'll see its power over you diminish like the incredible shrinking man.

On the positive side, don't overrate excellent writing either. We can take that to an extreme, as well. There's a story, apocryphal or not, about Nobel laureate William Faulkner when he was a visiting lecturer at the University of Virginia. He asked an audience of eager students, "How many of you want to *be writers?*" They all raised their hands. He then asked, "How many of you want to *write?*" Very few raised their hands. This anecdote reminds us that we too often have this silly, romanticized notion of writing. We see it as some exciting undertaking done in Technicolor with a Gershwin soundtrack in the background, the writer sipping a fine wine (which, in truth, can only deaden the imagination into a drunken stupor) and perpetually residing in the grace of artistic flashes of brilliance. Pu-leeze. Writing is work. Save the studio ideals for your next romance novel or chick flick. But at the office, do the work.

You should always be prepared to answer the question "What are you writing?" The way to always have an answer is to have your documents scheduled in your planner. Leave some fudge time for yourself to make sure you get the job done as planned, and allow time for emergencies that are bound to happen. The Four Ds come in handy here.

No writer is an island. Writing on deadline is not up to you alone. You need the help of others to meet your commitments consistently. Keep in the loop everyone who needs to be in it. Share what's happening on your writing jobs, and talk up the problems you anticipate. Establish clear deadlines with your collaborators, keeping in mind the ten ways of being: *specific, realistic, responsible, diligent, alert, forgiving, critical, flexible, congratulatory,* and *proactive*—all adjectives synonymous with an in-charge writer. The respect you give and exude will command a respect in return, a respect that will honor commitments to you and defer to your opinions.

Talking deadlines is one thing; talking ability is another. Communicate openly with managers, subordinates, teammates, clients, and vendors about the roles and responsibilities of writing projects, assuming complete responsibility for more than your role and accepting equal blame for problems, even those you have not caused. Be willing to do at least 51 percent of any assigned project without complaint. All of these commitments will make you shine as a writer and make others quickly forgive and forget your increasingly rare missteps.

But don't let them forgive and forget too quickly. On any lost opportunity, whether it's a missed deadline or a weakly written draft, ask for specific feedback. If it's praise you're getting, ask why the writing merits praise; if it's negative criticism, ask for pointed criticism. Use the 16 elements from the 5-Minute, 10-Minute, and 20-Minute Fix as a practical guideline.

Finally, expect the unexpected. Without being paranoid, take nothing for granted. Understand that you and your collaborators are human, subject to human frailties and to constant correction. Such an attitude, if it's sincerely intended, will likely spread to everyone around you. Your writing speed is probably improving as you imagine such a world! It can happen. It's up to you.

Keeping It Really Real

While reading this book, you might have said, "Yeah, it's easy for Phil to say. He can write, I can't. . . . He has it made because he doesn't have 40 people to supervise . . . 60 people to support . . . 10 bosses to answer to . . . 80 clients to serve. Those things he called myths about Mopey Moe aren't myths at all; they're the real deal. He hasn't had to work in my environment. Why should I take him at his word that this stuff works?"

These skeptics often become the most ardent supporters of the ideas in this book. Because you may challenge the claims of *How to Write Fast Under Pressure*, you may be quick to dismiss the tips before ever giving them a chance. While I can't blame you for believing that you just can't get those writing jobs done on time after years of experience with missed deadlines, I can fault you for being dismissive based on two faulty premises: (1) that many past failures absolutely lead to future failures, and (2) that all successful writers have always been successful writers. So here I submit to you the observations of two people, each of whom has been in his line of business for more than a quarter-century.

The first is myself. Many people who review my accomplishments think that I am a bookish academic with little experience in the real world, whatever that means. Nothing could be further from the truth. Yes, I have a doctorate in education. True, I've written four books and dozens of published articles on effective writing in reputable newspapers, journals, and magazines. And, OK, I've taught on the college and graduate levels and in many Fortune 100 companies, as well as federal, state, and municipal agencies. My clients have included the most educated people in society, including scientists, physicians, attorneys, accountants, professors, and CEOs. But what nobody sees when they consider those accomplishments is the 6-year-old boy I once was who struggled with reading, the 11-year-old boy I became who hated reading, writing, and anything that didn't have to do with sports, and the 16-year-old boy who begged his parents to let him drop out of high school. Even after getting a college degree at the age of 23, I wasn't a true believer. I was already married and employed as a New York City cab driver. Feeling much like a Mopey Moe myself, I sarcastically said, "That bachelor of arts and 50 cents will get me on the subway." (That's what the New York City subway cost back then!) You would think the master's degree I earned three years later would have changed my mind. By then, my wife was pregnant with our first child, and I had received a promotion at my new job as a marketing director for a nonprofit agency. Still, I was cynical.

After attaining the master of science degree, I said, "That's it: I will never step foot in a classroom again." But six years later, I changed. The story behind that change is too long and too boring to tell. By then, I was 33 years old, a father of two girls, and on a mission to write and teach for a living, neither of which I had ever done. It was a slow process, but I began publishing regularly and spent seven more years in a university working toward a doctorate, which I achieved at the age of 45. When people say, "You are an intellectual," I've got to laugh. They don't know my anti-intellectual roots, and they have ignored the reality that there are many routes to writing excellence.

The second person provides a more compelling case for conditioning yourself to try some of the ideas mentioned in this book. He is Matthew J. Loscalzo, a long-time friend. As Executive Director of Supportive Care Medicine for City of Hope in Duarte, California, Loscalzo is a leading authority on pain management with administrative, clinical, and academic credentials from institutions such as the Memorial Sloan-Kettering Cancer Center, Johns Hopkins Oncology Center, Eastern Virginia Medical School, and the University of California San Diego Cancer Center. He has three decades of research and practical experience in dealing with patients and their families as they cope with terminal illnesses, and he has lectured around the world on palliative care. Listening to Professor Loscalzo is always a learning opportunity for me or anyone who cares to listen.

Loscalzo rarely sees patients in high spirits; on the contrary, he meets people who are either facing death or who love someone who is. "People dealing with grief will cry or get irritable and angry," he explains. "They don't sleep the same, they don't eat as well, they experience weight loss, and they feel stress in relationships that were previously meaningful. They get no enjoyment in life where they once did."

When it comes surviving the loss of a loved one, he does not believe in the adage "time heals." "Time won't heal all wounds," Loscalzo points out. "Sometimes, the grief can never be lessened." Compounding the challenge is that grief is all around us in varying degrees. "We live with grief all the time: when we notice a new wrinkle, when we have to deal with a boss who isn't as smart as we are. The greatest of all is losing a child we love."

What is an antidote, or at least a suppressant, to grief, the most significant crippler of productivity? "Getting the executive function of the brain active," says Loscalzo. The executive function is the part of the brain that controls emotions, organizes issues, and solves problems. It's the part of the brain that I have been trying to get you to tap into throughout this book. "Get back into your routine within a week," he suggests. "When you are confronted by another human being, you are impacted by them. It is inherently therapeutic. It gets you out of yourself to be helpful."

When coping with the demands of his own profession, whether that means dealing with an overload of grief from patients and their loved ones or with the pettiness of peers who are sniping over some imagined slight, Loscalzo says, "I go to an envelope I keep in my desk. It contains notes of appreciation from people for what I did to help them in a time of need. That's why the work I do is worth the grief I get." He also keeps index cards nearby for whenever a creative idea pops into his head. If you recall the tips in Chapter 4 about keeping a log and practicing planning and drafting, you can see that these practices are not so novel but in fact the standard operating procedure of many successful people.

Loscalzo urges people coping with grief to write. "You can break out of grief not by trying harder but by trying less. Try something different. Writing is also a way of fueling the executive function," he concludes. Authors like William Styron have dealt with grief by writing about it. (Read Styron's book *Darkness Visible: A*

Memoir of Madness for a compelling account on the manifestations of depression and the ways of dealing with it.) *Writing for Wellness: A Prescription for Healing*, by Julie Davey, discusses the therapeutic effects of writing for cancer patients. We looked at health issues in Chapter 5 of this book, and medical professionals like Loscalzo would stand behind the notion that writing does in fact promote positive effects on an individual's life. If for nothing else, then, try writing.

A Closing Thought: Remembering Your Heroes

As I consider DASH, the four legs of writing fast under pressure, three people who are models of machine-like writing efficiency come to mind: Harry Kamish, Santi Buscemi, and Caitlin Piccarello. All three came to me at different times in my professional development, so I like to think of them as important people who have spanned my entire professional career. They have inspired me to write as fast as I can.

I met Harry Kamish in late 1977, when I was working at my first job after graduating from college, an entry-level position for a nonprofit organization serving the developmentally disabled. Harry was born on October 10, 1910 (10-10-10). At the time, he was already 67 and retired from a career in the U.S. Postal Service. No one enjoyed a good laugh as much as Harry—even at his own expense. He liked saying, "God figured I wouldn't have much of a memory for numbers, so he gave me only one: 10!" He loved the track, losing more money there than he would ever admit. What was most unforgettable about Harry for me, an aspiring writer, was the way he steadily, patiently, and untiringly attacked the keys of his Remington manual typewriter until he finished his letter to the editor of the *New York Daily News, New York Post,* or *New York Times* on behalf of a piece of legislation that would enhance the quality of life for developmentally disabled individuals. As the chief information officer for the agency, Harry saw writing as a task of great integrity, and he took his writing responsibilities seriously. His vocabulary was stunning. For fun, I would open an unabridged dictionary and pull words to stump him. I never once succeeded. He had a journalist's obsession with the truth and never suffered the fraudulent, the pretentious, or the arrogant. I will always remember how supportive he was of my endeavor to create an in-house newsletter. He was generous in sharing his wisdom gleaned from years of editing newsletters with a national circulation. He was detailed, direct, and well intentioned in his criticism of my writing, never failing to offer alternative expressions for a mangled phrase or a poor word choice. He stayed with the organization well into his eighties, working nearly until the time of his death. Writing for the cause of the developmentally disabled was his lifework. Why would he want to retire from the perfect job, one that enriched his life and gave him a chance every day to enrich the lives of others, as he so often did? Thirty years ago, I wanted to become just like Harry; 30 years later, I still do. Harry has been gone from this earth for more than a decade now, but I still hear his creative guidance, gentle criticism, and abiding encouragement.

Unlike Harry, who was old enough to be my grandfather, Santi Buscemi is old enough to be my older brother. For many years, he was the chairman of the English department at Middlesex County College in Edison, New Jersey, where he still teaches. He is well known for the college textbooks he has authored and co-authored, notably *Writing Today, A Reader for Developing Writers, 75 Readings Plus,* and *The Basics: A Rhetoric and Handbook,* all published by McGraw-Hill, a giant in educational publishing. I first met Santi in 1988, 11 years after I met Harry, when I became a writing instructor at Middlesex. He was in his office typing the finishing touches for one of his books. His secretary wanted to introduce us, so I stepped into his office while he remained sitting and typing. He turned to me and said breathlessly, "Hi nice to meet you sorry I'm on a deadline," hardly missing a keystroke.

If I were less understanding or tolerant, I would have considered his greeting rude and insulting. Actually, I thought nothing of the sort. I so admired the way he was committed to meeting a deadline and, frankly, a bit envious that at the moment I didn't have any exciting writing deadlines myself. No wonder McGraw-Hill has kept returning to Santi for more books. He is dedicated, focused, and committed. And Santi proved over and again to be a gracious, generous soul. He provided good counsel to me as a writing teacher, providing an important letter of recommendation on my behalf, and asked me to contribute to one of his electronic resources for English students. I had the great honor and pleasure some 10 years later of nominating him for an award when I was president of the New Jersey College English Association. For me, he will always be that guy rooted in his chair, not as a couch potato but as a productive writer sharing his wisdom with undergraduate composition students.

Another decade after leaving Middlesex, I was completing the first draft of this book, between Christmas and New Year's Day in the company of my wife and a house guest, Caitlin Piccarello, a young attorney who grew up as a close family friend. Caitlin was enjoying her free time with us, but she had to spend some time working on a legal brief that was due on January 15. She wanted to be done the first week of January so that the senior partner could provide his input and the secretary could convert the brief into the standard legal format. I was impressed with how Caitlin made sure she allowed plenty of time for the senior partner to review the brief so that they could all meet the deadline. But what really knocked me out was how this young woman, whom I've known since she was a babe in her mother's arms, typed nearly as fast as the speed of speech. Awesome! I wish I could do that! One more point: Caitlin told me that she doesn't necessarily enjoy writing, but this fact has not stopped her from doing what she has to do as a writer.

The thought hasn't escaped me that Caitlin was born 37 years after Santi and 71 years after Harry. They represent entirely different worlds as writers. Harry was slower but steady, artistic, and purposeful, getting the job done on his own schedule and in his own inimitable style. Santi is workmanlike, focused, and tireless, closing one deal just to open another, writing to meet no standard but his own, which is higher than that which anyone else would place on him, anyway. Caitlin is a fantastically fast writer, alternately rhythmic and sporadic, not enamored of writing but unafraid of it, accepting it for what it is and tackling it head on. As different from one another as they are, Harry, Santi, and Caitlin have something in common: They get the job done and on deadline. There are many ways to write in a heartbeat. Each of these people would subscribe to entirely different practices that are uncovered in these pages. If you admire any writer the way I do Harry, Santi, and Caitlin, then you'll find some practices in this book suitable to you too.

Now do it.

Index

Index

Index

Index

Index

Loscalzo, Matthew J., on grief and writing, 180–181

managers
criticism by, 137
editing by, 93
recognition of improvement by, 92
setting expectations with, 162–163
tips for, 27–28
Mandel, Barrett J., 101
Mann, Thomas, 13
A Manual for Writers of Research Papers, Theses, and Dissertations, 104
mapping your ideas, 51–52, 169
Mavis Beacon Teaches Typing (software), 113
meeting announcements, 48
meeting minutes, 15
meeting summaries, 41, 45
mental issues, in writers' worlds, 25, 103–109, 119, 173
Michener, James, 112
Microsoft, 96
The Mind Map Book (Tony and Barry Buzan), 52
Mindmapping (Joyce Wycoff), 52
minutes, meeting, 15
MLA Handbook, 104
modeling, productivity and, 117, 174–175
Mondrian, Piet, 101
monitors, flickering of, 96
Morrison, Toni, 97
motivation, for writing, 13–21, 168–169
Murray, Donald, 33
music, productivity and, 97–98
myths, about writing, 11–13, 17–19, 168

New York Times Manual of Style and Usage, 105
Nietzsche, Friedrich, on corruption, 102
noise, productivity and, 97–98
note-taking, 109–110

Oliu, Walter E., 32–33
On Creativity (David Bohm), 147

organizational ergonomics, 99–100
other writers
comparisons to, 77–78
spending time with, 115–116, 174
over-romanticizing, of writing, 77

Paine, Lauran, 112
The Paris Review Interviews (Paris Review), 146
path, in Three Big Questions, 23
Peale, Norman Vincent, 106
personal items, in work areas, 103
physical ergonomics, 98, 99
physical issues, in writers' worlds, 109–115, 119, 173–174
Piccarello, Caitlin, 184–185
Pinter, Harold, 13
planning, 169
and drafting, 76
for fresh writing, 61–62
and productivity, 113–114
when to skip, 61–62
in writing process, 35–37
Plimpton, George, 107
policies, templates for, 45
posting, 52–54, 169
preparation, for writing, 31
proactiveness, about deadlines, 159
procedures, writing about, 41, 45, 51
productivity
and beauty/art, 101–102
and clutter, 100–101
and drafting, 113–114
and duration, 111–112
and eating, sleeping, and exercising, 114
and electronic resources, 105–106
and ergonomics, 98–100
and grief, 180–182
and lighting, 95–96
maintaining steady flow of, *see* health
and modeling, 117
and noise/music, 97–98
and note-taking, 109–110
and planning, 113–114

Index

Index

About the Author

For more than 25 years, Philip Vassallo has taught writing in business, governmental, and academic environments; evaluated the writing of thousands of professionals across the entire spectrum of the organizational hierarchy; and developed writing training programs for a wide range of administrative, technical, and managerial professionals throughout the United States. He has also provided individualized writing coaching and assessment services for numerous corporate employees. His book *The Art of On-the-Job Writing* provides the groundwork for writing effectively and efficiently regardless of the writer's position, and his book *The Art of E-Mail Writing* provides numerous tips for writing focused e-mail. Phil is also an essayist, poet, and playwright. He holds a bachelor's degree in English from Baruch College, a master's in education from Lehman College, and a doctorate in educational theory from Rutgers University.